Life on the Fringe

Life on the Fringe

Testimonies of Women Living Beyond Desperation to Faith

JOAN McCLENDON & JAIMEE BINGLE

Library of Congress Control Number: 2012919950
ISBN-13: 978 0692446539

Life on the Fringe, Inc.
www.LifeontheFringe.org

First Evangel Press printing 2012
www.EvangelPress.com

ENDORSEMENTS

The Gospel of Mark tells us about a woman who is healed after touching the garment of Jesus. Enter into the story of 'Veronica' whose name means 'true image' and share the journeys of modern-day women who face their own brokenness to discover the healing that God's love offers.

TERI NICHOLAS
South Bend, Ind.

Both men and women need to read the stories in this book, and accept the invitation to touch and be touched by the Healer from Nazareth. These are inspiring stories of pain and triumph from courageous women whose voices need to be heard. We owe a debt of gratitude to them for being willing to share and for the editors in their vision to bring this angelic chorus to our ears.

DAVID MCCABE, PH.D.
Assistant Professor of New Testament,
Bethel College, Mishawaka, Ind.

Jaimee Bingle and Joan McClendon have crafted an incredibly beautiful book. Through their life stories and those of dozens of other women, you will be taken on a journey of faith, forgiveness, and hope. Read it and be transformed!

CHAD MEISTER, PH.D.
Professor of Philosophy and Theology,
Bethel College, Mishawaka, Ind.

Our testimonies of healing, and hoping in our Savior on the journey toward being healed, are powerful not only for building each other up in our "most holy faith," but in trusting Him that even our brokenness is precious, and something that He can use in our lives to bring us closer to His love. That's what this book speaks to all of us.

KANDA SNYDER
South Bend, Ind.

To all the courageous women who wrote for this book and the women who will be inspired by it. We believe these testimonies will be an invitation for others to receive a breakthrough in their own healing process.

TABLE OF CONTENTS

Acknowledgements 11

Preface 13

Introduction. 15

Part 1: A Tale of Two Women

Chapter 1: Keeping Hope Alive by Joan 23

Chapter 2: The Woman's Story 35

Chapter 3: Beauty in Suffering 43

Chapter 4: The Witness Protection Program 53

Chapter 5: Restoration. 65

Part 2: The Women's Stories

Chapter 6: Surrender Heals Broken Marriage by Micle 79

Chapter 7: Sustained by Joy by Ashley 83

Chapter 8: Darkness Exposed; Exchanged
for Truth, Light and Life by Sofia. 87

Chapter 9: Healed Through Prayer by Tamera 93

Chapter 10: His Perfection Covers Me by Erin 95

Chapter 11: The Heart of a Mother; a
Restored Family by Nickolette 99

Chapter 12: Through Life's Struggles,
God Breaks Through by Peggy 103

Chapter 13: Honor Restores Father-Daughter
Relationship by Trecia. 107

Chapter 14: Beauty in Brokenness by Deanna 113

Chapter 15: Have Faith, With God Anything
Is Possible in Marriage by Jennifer 119

Chapter 16: I Am Beautiful by Grace J. 125

Chapter 17: Brokenness Brings
Transformational Healing by Carol 129

Chapter 18: The Journey of Life by Janet 133

Chapter 19: Healing, Testing and Gold Teeth by Londa...................... 137

Chapter 20: Reaching for the Bible Instead of the Bottle by Julie Ann........ 143

Chapter 21: From Torment to Truth by Kelly 149

Chapter 22: The Princess and the Toad by Isla Grace........................ 155

Chapter 23: Rescue Me by Sarah... 159

Chapter 24: Learning to Be Still by Lydia.................................. 165

Chapter 25: Learning to Emerge by Linda.................................. 167

Chapter 26: Somebody Please Love Me by Nancy............................171

Chapter 27: Life Lessons in Courage and Faith by Gail 175

Chapter 28: Eczema and God's Healing
Through the Eyes of a Young Lady by Moriah............................... 179

Chapter 29: Making Good Choices by the Grace of God by Myra............. 183

Chapter 30: The Promise of Faithfulness, Strength and Love by Christal 187

Chapter 31: Looking for Peace in All the Wrong Places by Alisa..............191

Chapter 32: Broken-Hearted But Renewed By Him by Jaimee............... 197

Chapter 33: The Light of a Child by Melodie............................... 201

Chapter 34: I Have a Reason to Sing. I Have
a Reason to Worship by Assumpta...205

Chapter 35: A Chocolate Healing — My
Personal Journey From Bitterness to a Sweet Peace by Linda.................211

Chapter 36: Here I Am To Worship by Katie 215

Chapter 37: The Golden Ticket by Stephanie............................... 219

Chapter 38: Fresh Not Plastic by Terri 225

Chapter 39: Tainted Blood by Laura 229

Chapter 40: Forgiving Myself by Lily 235

Chapter 41: The Narrow Path by Emily....................................241

Chapter 42: Living an Authentic Life in the Image of God by Elizabeth.......247

Epilogue 257

End Notes..261

Acknowledgements

Thank you Jesus, you are the reason why this book exists.
We both thank you for the vision you gave us and the passion
to pursue and finish this project.

There have been a number of significant people I know that were sent by God to pray, encourage, challenge and help me on my journey.

Thank you to my wonderful husband, Cary McClendon, for your steadfast love and dreaming with me. To Joshua and Moriah, my super cool kids, thank you for being my biggest fans. I love you dearly.

Londa Harwell, I thank God for you. You are an example of a Godly woman and your wisdom is priceless! Thank you for choosing to roll in the mud with me.

Thank you to my spiritual mentor, Pastor David Hanson, for sharing your wisdom with me.

Thank you to Dr. Chad Meister and Dr. David McCabe for your patience, encouragement and wisdom. We appreciate your devotion to this project.

Joan McClendon

Thank you to my husband, Nathan Bingle. You have encouraged me and supported me through this whole process. Thank you for believing in me.

Thank you to the Bethel College marketing and communications office: Lissa Diaz, Matt Esau, Erin Kinzel, Katherine Ross and Becky Schaut. You encouraged Joan and I to take this dream farther. You gave your time and talents generously.

Jaimee Bingle

Preface

This is a book of stories from woman who have received healing through Jesus Christ. It is divided into two parts. In part one, the first chapter contains Joan's story. It is her testimony in her own words. The next chapter is a fictional account, based off scriptures from the Bible about the woman with the issue of blood. We used what we know about her from Matthew 9, Mark 5 and Luke 8 to secure the foundation of the story. Then we built on that with dialogue and emotion, all while trying to maintain truth about her culture, geography and time period. For example, since she wasn't given a name in the Bible, we named her Veronica in the story, which was a common female name in those days.

We added the historical fiction part because we wanted to paint a picture of what her life would have been like, what she might have felt, how she might have coped with her circumstance. Through this fictional story, it is our hope that you relate to this woman. Although she lived in another time period, culture and country, we don't think it will be hard for you to feel her pain, loss of identity and rejection. Why? Because wounds like these share no boundaries in life. Our stories may be different, but pain is pain no matter how, when or why you encounter it.

In addition, you'll find the remaining three chapters in part one include commentary and research about the woman's story, written from Joan's perspective. Topics include suffering/healing, identity, community and restoration.

In conclusion, we added questions for thought. Take some time to review the story and the message in each chapter. For example, if you struggle with your identity, ask the Lord to show you who you are. If you struggle with rejection, ask the Lord to show you what His acceptance looks like. Let Him heal you in the way He wants to heal you. Don't worry about somebody else's path to healing. Develop a deeper level of intimacy with Him while using this book as a tool to help you overcome your struggles and ultimately become victorious in Him.

In part two of this book you will find a different woman's testimony in each chapter. These are real women from northern Indiana and southwestern Michigan. Some of their names have been changed because of the sensitivity of their stories. Be encouraged as you read each testimony. Know that what God does for one, He can do for another.

Joan McClendon and Jaimee Bingle

Introduction

I was in the Spirit on the Lord's Day, and I heard behind me a loud voice like the sound of a trumpet saying, "Write in a book what you see ..." Revelation 1:10, 11 NASB

In December of 2010, I was worshipping at church when the Lord gave me a vision for a book that would be filled with women's testimonies. While it wasn't vivid and audible like's Apostle John's encounter, it was a soft inner-knowing, a vision inside my heart.

I have to say that at first I thought it was a little generic. I mean, aren't there books out there like that already? In my mind, that would never work. Who would share their story with me? And why would they want to do that? Plus, what publisher would print this book? So I tucked the thoughts away, repented for thinking God was generic and continued worshipping.

It wasn't until my close friend, Joan McClendon, called me the next day, super excited to tell me about a vision she had at church. I remember sitting on the other end of the line, jaw dropped, waiting to get a word in. Joan was rattling off the exact same thing I heard from God the day before. I couldn't believe it; two friends having the same vision at the same time. This squashed my former thoughts of a generic idea. I immediately shared my vision with Joan. We squealed with delight and hooped and hollered. We were going to write a book! It really was a simple decision.

You have to admit, it's a pretty cool confirmation. And it's definitely the foundation we needed and would remember over and over when our human nature got in the way, when we wanted to quit, or when we didn't believe. We were to carry this vision out together in an act of obedience, trusting the Lord through the whole process. We just knew His hand was in this project, and we believed He was going to provide the resources for us to carry out this vision. So after the squealing died down on the phone that day, the journey began to find women who had a testimony of the Lord working in their life.

Joan had been studying the woman with the issue of blood shared in Matthew 9, Mark 5 and Luke 8 for several years, mainly because she related to this nameless woman's story as she pursued her own path of healing. We knew this nameless woman's story would be the central theme to link all the stories of God's faithfulness together. Joan's study would be the springboard for the book.

As we scrolled through our Facebook friends, searching for intriguing Christian women with a story, we made a list of about 50 ladies that we knew in the region, who lived in southwest Michigan and northern Indiana. We also wanted as many women as possible from different cultures, age groups and church denominations to be represented. Each woman was to write their testimony and submit it to us.

We were overwhelmed with the responses. Many said that the Lord had already been speaking to them about sharing their testimony, but didn't know where they would do it. Others felt that sharing their story would be the closing chapter in their healing. Some told us of others that they knew of who had a great testimony. We contacted those women, without knowing anything about them, asking them to respond. And they did! You'll find nearly 40 testimonies in this book!

I received the first testimony from my dear friend, Micle. I had tears in my eyes as I read through her amazing story of how the Lord restored her marriage. I had known very little about this part of her life. In her story, she was so transparent and real. She held nothing back, exposing lies and deceit and proclaiming the healing power and goodness of God. It was beautiful. It was powerful.

I recognized at that moment that there are people in our lives that we meet for coffee, hang out with on the weekends and basically share life with, but we never know everything about them. Often, we miss the part of their life that has been challenging and now beautiful, or what has scarred them for life. Sometimes those details just aren't discussed. And sometimes that's a shame, because we can learn so much and be encouraged by each other; just knowing that somebody else has been on the same path can be reassuring. It's nice to know we're not alone in our struggle.

Many who read the testimonies in this book may think these women are brave — and they are. I'd go one step further and say they're free. When you are free you have nothing to hide. The memories are still there, but the pain is gone. The enemy always wants to keep things hidden so we can sit in pain. But the Lord wants to expose the darkness and reveal truth. In that, we are set free. Our testimony can help expose the darkness in someone else's life and bring truth to it as well.

Everybody has a story, and sharing the story of Jesus in your life is powerful. What He does for one person, He can certainly do for you.

Revelation 12:11 says:

And they overcame him because of the blood of the Lamb
and because of the word of their testimony. NASB

Who did they overcome? Him — the enemy or Satan.
How did they do that? By the blood of Christ and their testimony.
If you are seeking victory in the area of affliction, suffering, life's
circumstances, etc., you can overcome it with the Lord at your side!

As the stories rolled in, I continued to be even more amazed at the
goodness of God shown through these women's lives. Women wrote
about the guilt from abortion, sexual abuse, loss of a child, physical
healing, deliverance, freedom from addiction, restored marriage, wrong
mindsets, and the list goes on. While I couldn't relate to each woman's
specific wound because of a lack of experience, I could relate to her pain.
Haven't we all experienced pain on some level, whether it's physical or
emotional? That is one thing that we all have in common — the ability to
feel pain. What we may not share is the same path of healing or even a
complete healing. I believe we are all on a journey. We are "in process."

Joan and I are both still "in process." While we have experienced
levels of healing from the Lord, we have two totally different stories of
brokenness. The way we encountered God's healing in our own lives is
just as different. It's the same God, but the way His love responds to us
is unique to how He created us. You'll find that in each shared testimony,
the way each woman experiences God's healing is distinctive.

From the very beginning we knew this book was more than just a
book, but a platform for women to have a voice to share the goodness of
God. That's why we preserved the voices of the women who shared their
stories. As a writer, I wanted to tweak and rewrite and then make sure
every single sentence was perfect, but I felt the Lord telling me to give
these women a voice in the purest sense. In some stories, like Sophia's
for example, because I know her, I can totally picture her telling her
story just the way she wrote it. I think it's more powerful than what my
subjective editorial style could give it.

Joan and I also believe that the testimonies in this book will release
healing for many women in this region, and it will spread across the
nation and the world.

I know these women's stories will encourage you to keep on the path
of your own healing, and to trust in the Lord when circumstances seem
impossible. The woman with the issue of blood was in a seemingly
impossible situation; the doctor's remedies didn't work and she had

spent all she had. In fact, she had gotten worse. But she knew that if she could just touch the fringe of Jesus' robe, she'd be healed. And she was!

Coming up behind Jesus, she touched the fringe of His robe.
Luke 8:44 NLT

The idea around the title of this book, "Life on the Fringe," is the image of the woman grasping to touch Jesus' cloak. Can you picture the woman desperate to get near to Him, pushing her way through a crowd of people just to touch the fringe of His robe? In this book you'll find many testimonies of women who are also, desperate for a touch, even if it's just Jesus' robe.

Have you ever felt that way, desperate to touch Jesus, knowing that if you did, you would be healed? Well, keep the faith if you haven't received your healing yet. It is His will that you are healed. And be encouraged, you are not alone in your quest for complete wholeness. Just remember that you don't have to be 100 percent whole to have a testimony. You can give Him thanks even in the midst of your process. We encourage you to share your testimony with others, because if Jesus is in it, we know it's powerful.

Jaimee Bingle

PART 1
A Tale of Two Women

— CHAPTER 1 —

Keeping Hope Alive

BY JOAN

My journey with the Lord began with hope.

It was the summer of 1988. I was a 21-year-old college student on break visiting my oldest brother in Minneapolis. To make extra spending money, I worked at a daycare and cleaned offices at a local hospital.

I had flirted with the possibility of becoming a Muslim, just like my brother. He was deeply committed and seemed like he was fulfilled in his faith. After all, he did make it out of our chaotic, violent upbringing and seemed fine. I made it out of there too, but the problem was I wasn't fine. I was a mess. I knew it, and I needed help. I'd tried counseling, prescription pills, drugs and alcohol to ease the pain. Nothing worked.

As a child, I had attended church sporadically with my mother, but it didn't stick with me. I knew about God, but I certainly didn't know Him. That would soon change.

It was during my janitorial job at the hospital that I met a Christian woman named Erika. We connected immediately and met regularly on my break in her office. When we met she would encourage me to share my story. I was afraid because for the first time in my life, someone was genuinely interested in hearing about me. This woman acted like she was sincerely concerned about me and the condition of my heart.

Reluctantly, shared my past with her, and she listened attentively and respectfully. To my surprise, she invited even longer and more engaging conversations, sometimes meeting after work.

She pursued me, loved on me and ,most importantly, she never judged me. Later in one of our long discussions, Erika revealed that we had a lot in common growing up. She too had a rough childhood as a victim of abuse. The difference in our stories was that she was healed from her past. She didn't have to say it; she wore it all over her. I knew she was healed because peace radiated from her and I wanted to get closer.

I will never forget the day she said to me, "Joan, Jesus will take all the pain away if you let him."

I gasped and my knees buckled. I was startled by her remarks. I thought, is it possible? Could this be the hope that I so desperately needed and had pursued all my life?

I eagerly replied, "Really?"

She nodded her head.

I agreed quickly and we walked together to the hospital's chapel. We sat on a pew and she put her arm around me, held my hand and opened her Bible to Romans 10:9.

That if you confess with your mouth Jesus as Lord, and believe in your heart that God raised Him from the dead, you will be saved. NASB

The issues that I had struggled with for so long now had an answer. For me it was simple; I just needed to ask Jesus to come into my heart and believe that He would. As soon as I did this, I had a warm feeling sweep over me. I wept and wept until it was time to leave. I knew that something changed inside of me. Though I didn't have the full understanding of what happened, I felt cleansed and refreshed. Hope filled my heart! This was the start of my journey toward healing.

Growing Up in Philly

I struggle with remembering a time of feeling loved by my father or by anyone in my family. That doesn't mean that he didn't love me, or that they didn't love me, but that's just how I felt growing up. I carried a belief in my heart that I was unlovable. Even though my parents tried to express their love in their own way, I still perceived that I was unloved by them. This was especially true about my dad. He often seemed very unhappy. I remember from time to time we would do a few fun things like fishing, listening to Frank Sinatra and taking trips to the flea market in south Philly.

I also remember him singing to me, "Here she comes, Miss America."

When I think of that song, played during the Miss America Pageant, it brings a smile to my face. I remember watching the yearly televised pageant with my family. In this particular memory I was walking down the stairs pretending to be a beauty queen.

My father would clap as I did my pageantry wave. The attention that he showed toward me made me feel good about myself. Unfortunately, that is one of only a handful of times that I can remember him showing me, or any other member of my family, healthy affection.

We were a middle class family living in Philadelphia, Pa. I was the third child out of four. I was told by different family members how my dad was never excited about fatherhood. I wasn't surprised, knowing a little of his history. He grew up with an absent father and lacked a male role model. As an adult, he served in the military and was promoted to sergeant first class. After the military, he worked hard and was a great financial provider for our family. But he also was an angry alcoholic who yelled — a lot.

My father was often unpredictable. I grew up feeling like he was going to kill us. I lived in fear every day. He was intimidating, making many threats toward family members. There was another fear that I carried inside me. I feared his touch. Yes, my father on occasions had touched me inappropriately. I felt trapped because I believed that if I told anyone, more violence would break out. So I kept this secret in me to protect my family. The problem with secrets is that they breed and feed in darkness. As an adult, I realized that I didn't protect anyone by keeping my secret. I was deceived. It proved to be especially harmful to me, but I will go into that later.

Even the sound of my father's voice was enough to get me upset. When he yelled, his voice reminded me of thunder and I was terrified of it. I carried this fear into adulthood; even to this day, I still tremble when I hear a thunderstorm. I was especially afraid when he came up the stairs. He was the only one who would hit the top step right where it would creak. That sound triggered something in me that brought on fear. Later in life, doctors would diagnose me as hyper-vigilant, which is a disorder associated with extreme trauma and stress.

I remember one Christmas day as being the tensest time in our household. There was fighting and arguing. My oldest brother tried to smooth things over by telling us stories about Santa to comfort us. He was everything my father wasn't, and so I looked up to him. I also looked to him for protection when things were bad at home, though I could never tell my brother about my secret. So I kept my mouth shut.

My mother even had to sometimes rely on him for protection from my dad. Despite her hard work in the home and successful career, it was never enough. My father beat her, one time sending her to the hospital.

Of course with such a poor example of fatherly love and an environment that thrived on violence, all of us took part in negative behaviors toward each other, including me. This was our normal home life, many times acting like nothing was wrong. And on top of that, everything was a secret. No one was to ever know what was going on in our home, but we deceived ourselves; people knew. No one ever talked about it though. They simply opened doors for us to come in, put their arms around us and loved on us. I remember wanting to talk to someone so badly; it was tormenting, but I wasn't brave enough to share my secret with anyone.

That's probably why I had very few friends growing up. I couldn't go anywhere and the one or two friends I did have could rarely come over. I felt caged in a prison cell of fear, penned up with violence and anger with no way out. This was my life as a child in Philly.

My Safe Places

I don't want to paint the picture that every waking second was bad because that just isn't true. However, I carried the negative emotions and wounds everywhere, even to my "safe" places.

I can remember summers with my aunt and uncle in Nottoway, Va. I couldn't wait to get to their little farmhouse with my three siblings. Their home was so secluded with the nearest house miles away.

There we woke up to sunshine and acres upon acres of vegetation and fruit trees. Those fruit trees produced the most fragrant fresh air. I just loved that beautiful air and the feeling of peace, away from the chaos in my home.

We were on a farm, so there was work to be done, and I didn't mind helping my uncle milk cows and tend to the gardens. I especially loved chasing the pigs and the piglets in their pen playing "Adam 12," an old cops and robbers show from the 1960s. My uncle taught us how to pick ripe fruits and vegetables, which I enjoyed eating right on the spot.

I loved watching my aunt cook. Everything she made was from scratch, even butter and ice cream. She even killed her own chickens. She taught me how to appreciate nature, hard work, determination and the peacefulness that came by being alone. I would often catch her sitting on their screened-in porch humming hymns and reading her Bible. My siblings and I would venture off to explore on the farm; sometimes we would stay out all day.

My other safe place was about 15 minutes away from my home.

Just about every weekend my family (everyone but my dad) would visit my Aunt Marguerite's, where she and my Uncle Johnny lived in a huge, three-story home, in what I perceived as a mini-mansion. There were tons of great places to hide and be alone in their home. We had a wonderful time playing games with my cousins and laughing, and I just loved being with my extended family. There was so much expressed love. My aunt and uncle made me and anyone who visited feel special.

I recollect wanting to spend the night with our cousins at their house, but for the most part, my father would often forbid it. From time to time I did get to stay, but it caused big fights between my mother and father. Everything was controlled by my dad. Eventually he would end all sleepovers completely.

I can recall each time going back home to our house, getting into the car and shaking uncontrollably all the way home. I was afraid because I knew what was coming when we got there, and there was no way to prepare for or protect myself from it. The inevitable was the greeting from an angry and unpredictable father. It was almost unbearable, because many times my emotions would spin completely out of control. Eventually, I taught myself how to suppress my emotions. I did this well, but in the end, I developed more problems; this time it was a nervous stomach from all the stress.

Breaking Free from my Home Life

I was ashamed of my home life and myself. In fact, I hated myself. The abuse forced me to put up walls of self-protection. Fear was a constant, even after I moved out of my parents' house.

I continued to carry the biggest lie — that nobody loved me. The best way that I can describe that feeling is a gaping hole like an empty abyss. So in high school I went looking for love. It was like my desperation for love was magnified. I had no clue what it looked like. I had some ideas, but they were distorted views based on TV shows. Eventually I would get into a destructive relationship where I was introduced to drugs and alcohol. I knew in my mind that this relationship was wrong, but I continued in it because it fed my deep woundedness and the longing to be loved. I was deceived, not even realizing that this toxic relationship had inflicted even more pain in my life.

On high school graduation day I felt like I was handed the keys to freedom. I no longer had to sit in the cell called home, though I was still too young to realize that I was not free at all because I was still locked up inside. I would eventually learn that my mess traveled. I had become an expert at packing my mess, stuffing it, picking it up and moving it from place to place. I would carry this to college and subsequently, everywhere I went.

At college I was partying and "living it up." Essentially, I was self-medicating. It was the new way I found to deal with the pain. I was flunking out of college, and in some twisted way I wanted to flunk out. But there was one thing that stopped me from doing that. I knew that if I didn't succeed here, I'd have to go back home and I was not going to let that happen. So I tried counseling and stopped drinking, hoping that would help ease my pain. It helped for a short period of time, but eventually I reverted back to finding unhealthy methods of ending my pain.

Attacks on My Life

As if my messed-up emotions couldn't get worse, I started to experience unfamiliar emotional outbreaks. Everything that was buried inside me started to manifest on the outside. I would later find out these were panic attacks.

The first time I experienced a panic attack, I was walking around an expo in Monroeville, Pa. There were hundreds of people walking around me and I felt faint. I started sweating and the room felt like it was closing in on me. It was just too much for me. I had this uncontrollable fear, and I needed to get out of there quickly.

I also struggled with suicidal thoughts. My first attempt happened when I was a junior in college, just months before I gave my life to Jesus. I tried to walk in front of a bus. I don't know why. It's like a feeling came over me and I wanted to hurt myself; I just needed the pain to go away. The pain was not superficial, but it came from a deep place within me, my abyss. Deceitful thoughts told me it would be pleasurable to hurt myself. There was no sadness involved either. I just wanted to die.

It didn't happen though; God had another plan. I believe this was my first God-experience. I had just ended my shift at a store in the mall and was waiting for the bus to take me back to my residence hall on campus. I don't know why, but I was very relaxed when I chose to step in front of the bus as it pulled up. That's when a woman came from out of nowhere knocked me down to the ground and stood on top of me.

She said, "You know, Jesus loves you."

It was winter-time and she was a heavy woman with short, dark hair wearing shorts. She didn't say anything else, but then turned to walk away, leaving me on the ground. I watched her for as far as I could and I never saw her again. I believe that God sent an angel down from Heaven to save my life that day.

This incident set me on a path. On that day I realized that there was an enemy that wanted to destroy me, though I didn't know who that enemy was. God showed me that there was a battle going on for my life, but even more importantly, He showed me that He loved me and would fight for me.

When I became a Christian, I found that there is an enemy on a mission who seeks to kill, steal and destroy. His name is Satan. But God is on a mission as well, to reveal Himself to me intimately so that I may have victory over Satan. As I gave myself over to studying the Bible and committing to regular church fellowship, I grew stronger and wiser. Little by little I realized I wasn't fighting this battle alone.

The Stirring for Healing

The next part of my story paints a seemingly beautiful life that most girls dream about. In many ways it is ideal.

I was married in 1992 to a wonderful, godly man named Cary. We soon had two beautiful children, Joshua and Moriah.

In the corporate world, Cary would climb the ladder and I'd go on to own a cleaning business. We soon gained a comfortable lifestyle, great friends, leadership in the church and ministry opportunities in the community.

Anyone who looked at my life could see the goodness of God around me. But God wanted to give me more than stuff and success; He wanted to heal me. I was never satisfied with only the outward goodness; I wanted the inner goodies too: peace, joy, longsuffering and love!

What it all boiled down to was that first day I met Jesus in the hospital. On that day I received my salvation and believed that He would eventually heal me. I still had hope that it would happen.

Desperately Seeking

For years I kept desperately seeking healing. What I found out about myself was that I would get a measure of healing throughout the years, but I had a tough time keeping it. In 2010, while I was taking my last couple of classes before completing my first master's degree at Bethel College, it would all come to a head. At that time I was taking a course that seemed more challenging than any class I'd taken before. This class, combined with family life and other pressures, sent me into a deep depression. This time the depression was triggered by the fear of not succeeding. So as strange as it may seem, I went to that familiar place of self-protection.

It was in this place that I finally realized that no one was harming me more than myself. I was still dealing with old issues and unhealthy patterns from my past. You see, I had forgiven my dad for everything he had done to me and my family, but I recognized that I was still in process. I had let God take some of my mess — the torment in my mind and the ache in my heart — but not all of it.

At that point I knew that it was critical for me to resist the urge to go back to my familiar place, so I chose counseling. I prayed and the Lord led me to Voice Ministries in Elkhart, Ind. There I met an amazing woman named Londa Harwell. She leads the healing team there. She too, knows what it means to suffer. She has a powerful testimony about the Lord's healing in her life. (Read Londa's story in Chapter 20.)

For almost two years I would meet faithfully every week for sessions. The sessions were extremely exhausting and intense at times. All of the digging and dredging through memories of past wounds would sometimes make me become physically ill, but I was determined to get healing; no more hiding and stuffing for me! I was desperate to get to the root of these issues that were keeping me bound, robbing me from the fullness of Christ in my life.

The Healing Process

In my years of being a Christian, I have witnessed the miraculous where God has used me to lay hands on people. These people were healed or delivered of a variety of things in an instant through prayer. Personally, I have stood at the altar and received healing like that as well, but not always the way I wanted or expected it. What I do realize is that healing can come instantly or it can be a process. God is in both of them. When Jesus healed instantly in the Bible it was called a miracle. It was supernatural. For other healings that occurred, Jesus was in them, but sometimes it took it little longer. (Mark 8:23, 24)

I still believe that God can and wants to do instant healings. However, what happens when you don't get healed instantly in the way you think you should? For me, I wasn't discouraged, I just kept seeking healing. I know that God is my healer and healing is for me, but it's a longer journey. Today, I can say that I've learned and grown so much through my healing process, perhaps much more than if I were healed instantly. Let me share with you a few things.

1. HEALING IS A PROCESS

At the time of the printing of this book, I am not fully finished with my healing, though I believe that one day I will be fully healed and, quite honestly, whatever that looks like is changing every day. What I mean is that I'm slowly realizing that I am just a small part in God's bigger plan, and the more He reveals to me His plan for my life, the focus on my own healing becomes less. Please don't get me wrong. In no way do I want to stay where I am, and I know God's purpose in me is healing. But what if He doesn't heal me in the way I think He should? Do I become bitter?

I've had the privilege to interview most of the women who wrote for this book. And there are others who wanted to write, but are so entrenched in their own process that they are not in a place where they can write right now. One elderly woman who didn't write for the book shared her story with me.

She has suffered from partial blindness since she was in her late 20s. She told me how her blindness led her on a road of bitterness and resentment toward the Lord. She cried out for healing. It never came. One day she went to a healing crusade, once again with all her heart believing that she would receive healing of her sight. On that day, she received something more than what she could ever expect; God filled her with peace. And so this woman no longer complains about the fact that she cannot see, because on that day God caused her to "see" something far greater than healing in and of itself; she saw Jesus! When we get to "see Him," He becomes our focus, instead of the problem in front of us. Jesus is the focal point of our story.

As for me, there has been major progress. I'm not that same woman who began this journey two years ago. And because of that, my relationship with Him is deeper, richer and more intimate than ever, all because I chose to focus on Him.

2. LEARN YOUR IDENTITY

When everything gets shaken that needs to get shaken out of your life, you need to know who you are and whose you are. God wanted me to have an identity in Him, not in my brother whom I admire and not in my husband whom I adore. It's not in my mother, my counselor or even my wonderful aunt who provided a safe place for me as a child. My identity is also not in my wounds from my past because the mistakes of my past do not define me. Christ defines me. I wouldn't change anything about my life, even though I still struggle. I've learned that God loves me the way I am, even in my mess. He has been glorified in my weakness. Everything the enemy meant for harm and for my destruction, God has turned it around for good. God has been faithful.

3. DON'T GIVE UP – TRUST HIM

Every time I wanted to give up, I would go to the Lord and let Him reveal Himself to me in that area of weakness and I would not be afraid. In fact, I've learned that He loves it! He's not afraid of my mess no matter how bad I think it is. One of the greatest revelations I've received is that God speaks! I just needed to know how to listen to Him. I've also learned that when I trust God in the process, I will see fruit – good fruit. I made a choice; enough is enough. I laid all my chips on the table in surrender. There was nothing else in me. I realized that every time I would lay something down, God would quickly take it and give me something far greater in exchange. Sometimes it was revelation or a bit of wisdom, and sometimes it was just peace; His *shalom*. I would give Him my weakness and He would give me His strength. What does that look like? It is: love, confidence, trust, identity and lots of other great things.

4. IT'S ABOUT RELATIONSHIP

It's crazy, but healing is no longer my destination. It's important, but I'm enjoying God being revealed to me far more.

Earlier this year I was talking to a friend about her struggle with a certain situation. She was going through sleepless nights, bouts of anger and pure torment.

"Why won't God fix it? I love God," she said. "Why won't He fix it?"

I reminded her of one of her recent prayers, "God, make me more like you. Teach me how to draw close to you. I will give my life to you."

When you start praying like that, He will move in that direction and honor your prayer. It may not look like what you think it should. You may not step into your destiny right then and there, but you will go through the process of getting cleaned up and shaped into becoming like Him. He is ultimately trying to get His purpose out of us, and sometimes it doesn't feel so good. He's not a "give me this and give me that" God. Throwing a temper tantrum doesn't mean you get your way, but He will honor that original prayer and set you on a path toward healing.

I'm glad my friend was open to that word of advice. I can speak it confidently, knowing that I was in her place at one point. I wanted a bailout and a parachute, but I learned that healing wasn't coming any other way than through going deeper in relationship with Him and disciplining myself to sit in His presence.

I've also learned that my wounds aren't about a person, place or thing. It's not about what my father did to me, or even about what others did to me. It's what God is teaching me about what's inside my own heart. I can't go around blaming people for what's going on inside of me, but I can go to God. He can pinpoint what is my heart issue and bring healing, if I let Him. He will help me forgive. But I've got to keep myself in a place where I can hear His voice, or I know I'll miss it.

Pressing On

Looking back on my process so far, I'd say it was all worth it. I know when it's all said and done, it will still be worth it. I just keep giving little bits and pieces to Jesus as He reveals them to me. Each time I do that, He does a trade off with me. I found that the more healing I get, the more He does something really amazing in my life.

Through healing and relationship with God, He has given me boldness to overcome fear, and His love that overcomes shame. He has taught me about my identity, and that He is Lord of everything. I know that may sound sterile, but I mean it in a gentle and reverential way. It took a shift within me to be able to say that I can do nothing without Him, and that is a very good thing. He taught me to trust Him and lean on Him. It sounds generic, but with everything in me, I want to learn to trust Him. I found strength that came through surrender and complete dependency on the Lord.

I never would have imagined that I would be doing what I'm doing today, writing this book, working on a second master's degree, experiencing His love and the love of others around me. I believe it was the intention of the enemy to keep me silent in that place of shame, fear, anger, self-protection and self-hatred, but God had other plans.

He never forgot that day in the hospital's chapel in Minneapolis., when I gave my life to Him with the hope that He would heal me. I never gave up that hope and He didn't give up on me. It's that same hope that has now produced my faith for complete healing and wholeness in Him.

— CHAPTER 2 —
The Woman's Story

Then Jesus had crossed over again in the boat to the other side, a large crowd gathered around Him; and so He stayed by the seashore.

One of the synagogue officials named Jairus came up, and on seeing Him, fell at His feet and implored Him earnestly, saying, "My little daughter is at the point of death; please come and lay Your hands on her, so that she will get well and live."

And He went off with him; and a large crowd was following Him and pressing in on Him. A woman who had had a hemorrhage for 12 years, and had endured much at the hands of many physicians, and had spent all that she had and was not helped at all, but rather had grown worse after hearing about Jesus, she came up in the crowd behind Him and touched His cloak. For she thought, "If I just touch His garments, I will get well." Immediately the flow of her blood was dried up; and she felt in her body that she was healed of her affliction.

Immediately Jesus, perceiving in Himself that the power proceeding from Him had gone forth, turned around in the crowd and said, "Who touched My garments?"

And His disciples said to Him, "You see the crowd pressing *in on You, and You say, `Who touched Me?' "*

And He looked around to see the woman who had done this. But the woman fearing and trembling, aware of what had happened to her, came and fell down before Him and told Him the whole truth.

And He said to her, "Daughter, your faith has made you well; go in peace and be healed of your affliction." Mark 5:21 - 5:34 NASB

***

Veronica woke up to the bright rays of sunshine on her face, but she could barely sit up in bed to look outside her window and enjoy it. Right then she knew it was going to be another day of lying in her bed.

She had a small garden outside, but lately she couldn't give it the attention it needed to produce vegetables. Every time she would get out her garden tools, she would have to take a rest because she would feel weak and faint. Eventually she would end up back in the house, in her bed and hungry.

She mainly relied on her sisters to drop off a small loaf of bread and a jug of water a couple of times a week. They never visited long, but would exchange a few words, mainly town gossip, and then leave as quickly as they had come.

She'd been cooped up in her house for what seemed like days and she was getting tired of it. Her home had already turned into a prison and now she was confined to one spot — her bed; now the cell was a little bit smaller.

She wasn't sure how much of her actual sickness was making her tired and how much of it was the deep sadness that had recently settled in. It seemed she was now suffering from two diseases, hemorrhaging and depression, and it just kept getting worse.

Several months ago she had mustered up all her willpower, eaten a good breakfast of raison cakes and hoped with all her strength that the doctor she set out to visit could help her. It was her last hope of healing.

That hope was smashed to pieces when the doctor offered the same remedies that others before him had suggested.

"Take gum Alexandria, of alum, and of crocus hortensis, the weight of a zuzee each; then let them be bruised together and given in wine. Now if that doesn't work," the physician said. "Come back and I'll boil Persian onions in wine over nine logs. I'll have you drink the broth. Then I'll say to you, 'Arise from thy flux.'"

The doctor had assured Veronica that one of these would work, but she knew better. She tried both of these remedies many years ago and she became worse. She would never forget how heavy her flow became, she was faint for weeks afterward and missed working during harvesttime.

She would pass on this last remedy.

"Thank you," she mumbled.

Veronica picked up her walking stick. It was pointless telling the doctor that she had already tried that. Now she had to make it back home with a heavy heart and an illness.

Unfortunately, she also gave her last two coins for payment. Since she couldn't work, she knew the inevitable was upon her — begging. She'd either have to beg her father or the townspeople for money. She already decided years before that she would never do that. She couldn't beg. It was already embarrassing enough with her condition. She'd rather die. Redemption had to come some other way.

That day as she walked back to her small dwelling place, she cried out to God and believed for a miracle in her life.

"Lord, You are my healer. I am trusting in You and You alone. I have tried everything. Have mercy on me!"

After her prayer, Veronica had made up her mind that she would live off the land and hope. The God of Israel would help her. Perhaps He would send someone to visit her.

Now months later, little did she know that today would be the day. After 12 long years, she was about to get her healing and so much more.

***

Sometimes to keep her mind off of her condition, while she lay in bed, Veronica would daydream of what her life could have been. She would picture a hard-working, loving husband who adored her like how Jacob adored Rachel (Genesis 29:20). Then she would envision motherhood. She was hopeful that she would be a mother to many sons like Leah (Genesis 29: 32-35; 30:21). And just as she imagined the face of her first child, she would realize she was crying; crying because these were lost dreams. That's as far as her imagination could go before it ripped open all her wounds.

When she was 13, her father was making arrangements for her to wed. At that age she was barely a woman; she had just started her womanly flow. Now her father could prove to men that his daughter was of childbearing age.

Veronica's father was hopeful that he would be able to provide a fair dowry and perhaps a little less than normal. She had many qualities; she was strong, hard-working, a good cook and her sweet nature outshone the rest of his daughters. Her long flowing black hair, olive skin and big brown eyes caught the attention of several lookers. He would have no problem finding her a mate, or so he thought.

But when Veronica's menstrual cycle lasted weeks and then months, it made it difficult for her father to negotiate a dowry. No man wanted a woman who couldn't produce sons, let alone one that was constantly bleeding.

Her father tried everything: increasing the dowry, even offering to pay one possible groom's family double. He promised that this was no real concern and that his daughter would be well soon, but word had spread among their small community. Veronica was now off limits.

She knew she had brought deep disappointment and shame to her father when he stopped talking to her. All she wanted to be was a pleasing daughter, one who brought honor to her family, but she had failed. Veronica made a vow in her heart that she would never be a liability to anyone. It was time to leave her home and take care of herself.

Her hopes and dreams of being a wife and a mother were shattered. The day she left home, was the day that she accepted that reality. If she couldn't have children, she would have nothing and be nothing. She would hold no value to any man — even her father. She would just become another mouth to feed in his household, and someone to take care offor. She would live a lonely life with the identity of a childless woman who was sick and worthless to men.

She rolled over and pulled the thin sheet she used as a blanket over her head. The pain was too much to handle. Sleep couldn't come fast enough. That afternoon, Veronica awoke to the sound of shouting outside her window. It seemed like the whole town was running somewhere, but where? Veronica really wanted to ignore it, but she couldn't.

She pulled herself up and hung on to furniture as she made her way toward the door. She planned to take a small peek outside to see what all the commotion was about. Just as she opened the door, she saw a young boy coming toward her on the road.

"Where are you going?" she shouted.

He kept running, and as he passed her he said, "The Messiah is in town. I'm running down to the lake to see Him."

"What?" she said puzzled.

He was too far gone, racing down the hill toward the rest of the crowd that was forming by the lake.

Veronica closed the door. She had to process what this boy just said to her. Could it be? Jesus of Nazareth, the one everyone talked about, in her village? Was he really the Messiah? She may be a shut-in in her home, but she knew what was going on — thanks to her sisters who were the town gossips.

She had heard of a man named Jesus, who some claimed to be the Messiah. He had been visiting towns with his disciples, healing the sick, performing miracles and conversing with sinners.

While everyone was running to meet Him, she felt confined to this small hut. Today, her blood flow was heavy, and typically on those days, she steered clear of everyone b. ecause of her hemorrhaging, Veronica was considered unclean according to the law. That meant that if she sat on anything and bled through her clothes and soiled the seat, the seat would be unclean. If someone touched that seat, he or she would be considered "unclean" and have to wait until evening to be clean again. In Veronica's case, she was unclean all the time because her bleeding was constant.

While she could prevent this exchange by wearing extra linens, Veronica tended to be paranoid. She didn't want to be a threat to anyone and she internalized everything. If she was at the market, she felt like everyone was staring at her or snickering about her condition. It all stemmed from one incident more than a decade ago.

She would never forget the day she overheard several of her friends talking about her as she was coming up to join their conversation. It was during the time her fFather was seeking a mate for her.

"Did you hear about Veronica?" one of the girl's said.

"Yeah, she's unclean," another one of them piped up. "Who would want her as a bride? She's so dirty."

It was like a knife to her heart. Veronica cried for days. She finally came to the conclusion, that what they said was true. She was unclean.

But there was one thing no one could take away from her — the hope of the coming of the Messiah. It was the only positive thing that she believed. In the meantime, she would still uphold the law, and she would do a good job of it. Lawfully, she didn't have to remove herself from the community, but she wanted to be mindful of others and the possibility that she could make others unclean. She decided that she would remove herself from the community. That way the chances of her tainting anyone would be low. She would stay inside, venturing out only to go to the doctors who couldn't help her, and to tend her garden.

Now, for the first time in months, her heart leapt and suddenly she had strength. She would go see this Jesus. She got dressed and left her home, slowly making her way down the hill toward the large crowd she saw up ahead. There was no need to be discreet just yet, not a soul was around. They were all huddled together down at the lake. Jesus must be addressing them.

The closer she got, the more she realized that the group was moving. They were headed toward her. Her heart started beating faster. For the first time in a long time she didn't care if someone noticed her and started making fun of her; it would be worth it, especially if He really was the Savior.

Veronica quickly hid in an alley tucked back from the main road in the village. She was far enough away and yet close enough to see Jesus if He chose to walk this way. She offered up a quick prayer to the God of Israel.

"Lord, I'm desperate for a glimpse of Jesus. Let it be that my eyes gaze upon Him."

The closer Jesus and the crowd got, the more anxious she got. Was this really Him? Would He really save us all? Then she had a realization, if this really was the true Messiah, He could heal her. Suddenly, the possibility of healing increased her faith.

She knew the Messiah could heal her. She just had to get close to Him. Perhaps she could just touch Him. It seemed near impossible to do that, but she would try. She had to. And her chance was coming, the crowd was close. She could see His disciples making a way for Him, trying to keep people away so He could walk forward. They were seconds away from Veronica.

Veronica took a deep breath, pulled her cloak up around her face to hopefully hide her identity, and walked straight into the moving crowd.

There He was. She could see Jesus. He was so close. Right then, she got pushed to the side by the crowd.

"Make way for the Master. Give the man space," someone shouted.

Veronica started to lose her footing. She had very little strength and she was amazed that she even made it this far. But this was her chance. She thought to herself, grab hold of something, don't let yourself fall.

But the inevitable happened, Veronica fell to the ground. As she fell, she reached out her hands to grasp on to something, anything, but she couldn't. Now she was on the ground and some men were scurrying to pick her up and move her away. She couldn't move yet, she'd come this close. Quickly her eyes scanned for Jesus.

She saw Him, just as the men were lifting her up. Jesus was so close to her. She couldn't explain how she definitely knew it was Him, but she knew. It was like He was moving toward her. She reached out to touch Him, but only touched the fringe of His robe before the men lifted her up and set her to the side of the road.

Instantly Veronica's body felt different, and she knew she was healed.

She picked herself up and was prepared to head home, full of overwhelming joy. She would process everything that just happened, but that's when she heard Jesus call out.

"Who touched My garments?"

The crowd stopped. The disciples huddled around Jesus and said, "You see the crowd pressing in on You, and You say, `Who touched Me?'"

Jesus wouldn't let it go. He was serious. He wanted to know who touched Him. Actually, He knew who it was, but he wanted her to come to Him in front of the crowd. He had more in store for Veronica than just a healing.

She began to tremble with fear. Why had she touched Him? Why had she even left the house this morning? Now she would be shamed in front of everyone.

Veronica starting making assumptions; they spawned from negative thoughts that were bred from loneliness and self-imposed alienation. She thought the Savior was mad at her because she touched Him. But she was healed. Just from that little touch of His garment she felt a change inside of her. It was electric. Her mind went back and forth between joy and fear of being found out.

Veronica would stand up and take her fate no matter how horrible it was. She had taken something from the Master that she wasn't worthy to receive.

Right then Jesus noticed her. Veronica ran and fell before Him with fear and trembling and told Him the whole truth.

And He said to her, "Daughter, your faith has made you well; go in peace and be healed of your affliction."

She looked up at Him in shock. She couldn't believe what He had just said to her. Did Hhe just acknowledge her healing? Did He just call her,

"Daughter?" Her own father wouldn't even receive her, but this man calls her daughter in front of the whole town?

The tears poured out as she looked up at Him. His eyes were so tender and loving. No person had ever looked at her like this. She knew in her heart that He was the real Messiah.

That day she had received more th mainly because she related to this nameless woman's story as she pursued her own path of healing.ean she hoped for. She was healed. The bleeding stopped. The torment from the community stopped. They all knew she was different. She was no longer unclean. Jesus had made her clean again. He restored her and showed her worth to the townspeople. He adopted her as Hhis daughter and she could feel Hhis fatherly love. Now she could begin her life free from affliction, back in the community with a new identity — all because of the love from one man, Jesus the Messiah.

— CHAPTER 3 —
Beauty in Suffering

If you've given birth, you can probably relate to suffering.

With my first child, I was in labor for 36 hours. It was the most painful experience of my life, and I thought it would never end. On top of that, I had kidney stones. Between the two, I couldn't tell you which pain was worse.

I begged for pain relief and an epidural, but the doctor would not allow the epidural until I pressed through more pain. My cervix needed to dilate a little more. If they were to administer the drug too early it would slow down the birthing process, and I wanted nothing more than to get this baby out of me as quickly and safely as possible. I realized that I would have to wait and suffer through this pain a little longer, but this pain had purpose; a beautiful baby would eventually emerge.

Once I looked into my son's eyes and held him for the first time, the recent labor brought meaning and definition as to why I went through the process in the first place.

My suffering in labor lasted 36 hours and it was tough, but in life suffering doesn't always have a timeline. In childbirth, there is typically a promise of a child after the pain; a new life. In life's circumstances, we don't always know what the outcome will be.

In my personal story of healing, I still don't know the timeline, but I believe the outcome is going to be beautiful because of my faith in Christ. He makes all things new! (2 Corinthians 5:17)

I'm Broken and I Need Help

I've studied the story of the woman with the issue of blood in Mark 5 for the past four years. I identify with the woman because I, too, know what it means to suffer. There is so much to be said about this woman's story. Her story is not only a story about suffering, but it's rich with revelation about Jesus and the Kingdom of God.

In Chapter 1 you read my personal testimony about my abusive upbringing and my desperate need for healing. The woman and I both suffered in body, mind and emotions. Like the woman, I desired healing so much that I became desperate for it. Before I knew that Jesus was the one that I should be chasing after for healing, I used other methods to cope with the abuse. I managed to use creative methods of self-protection. One technique I developed was the ability to disconnect myself from bad things when they were happening to me. In a stressful or dangerous situation, I had the ability to allow my mind to check out. I felt very little or no emotion at all during this. It was my mind's way of dealing with the unpredictability and violence in my home and difficulties in life.

I carried this way of self-protection into my college years. Professionals have told me that if I didn't have this method in place, I likely wouldn't be here today. And I believe them.

This method worked and it was a great tool I used to help me survive, but it was unhealthy. It began to trickle into almost every aspect of my life. My academics began to suffer and because of my fear and mistrust of people, my relationships with friends were also affected.

I also suffered from depression and panic disorder, often avoiding difficult situations for fear that I would lose control. Though I taught myself how to behave like the good girl in relationships with family and friends. Again, this only complicated the problem. I needed to deal with the deeper issues, the root of the problem, anger and self-hatred. On the outside I was a loving and caring person, but on the inside, rage flowed through my veins.

I also struggled with the inability to express my true feelings. So I did the safest thing; I learned to hide my emotions, neatly sweeping them under the rug. If they would involuntarily leak out without my permission, I punished myself mentally, emotionally and sometimes even physically. It was tormenting.

Like the woman in Mark 5, I got to the point where I decided enough is enough! I'm broken and I need HELP! The Bible does not specify the nature of her bleeding issue, but it clearly states that she suffered with an issue for 12 years. This is a long time. It is a common belief that the woman's symptoms were related to her menstruation (this was the thought that we carried through in the fictional account), but it could have also been an issue that occurred from a previous pregnancy that was never healed. It isn't specified if she bled a lot or a little. Was her flow constant or did it occur intermittently? In reading her story there is evidence proving that this depleted her physically, mentally, financially and spiritually. We will delve into her struggles through the book.

Desperate People Do Desperate Things

Because of her great desire to be healed, she poured all of her financial resources and hope into her physicians. One interpretation, "The Adam Clarke Commentary," considers the therapeutics of the Jewish physicians in reference to hemorrhages, especially of the kind with which this woman was afflicted. You read a couple of the possible remedies in the fictional account. [1]

There were no distinct health care providers back then like there are today. Can you imagine a society with no doctors that specialized in women's care like an obstetrician or gynecologist? Even the procedures during that time were basic and hodge-podge. We'd laugh today if a doctor prescribed those medicines or procedures for us. But this woman was desperate and desperate people do desperate things. She wanted healing no matter what the cost. She kept trying until she exhausted all her resources.

Also similar to the woman, I spent a lot of money visiting many doctors and counselors, but the emotional pain persisted. My physician prescribed medication. Unfortunately, he couldn't offer a permanent solution for my condition. In many cases, emotional pain can be much more difficult to treat than physical pain. With physical pain you can point to what hurts. It's not the same for emotional wounds.

This type of pain has no scarring and is hard to pinpoint. For me, the medication was only a Band-Aid, not the answer I needed. Once again, I felt alone and ashamed, primarily because taking medications for emotions was a taboo subject back then.

Anyway, my so-called self-protection actually held me captive, a prisoner in my own cell, furnished with my own toilet to dump my mess in. The more I tried to suppress my mess, the smellier it became. The more I swept it under the rug, the more obvious it became. You can only bury so much under the rug without it eventually becoming noticeable. I realized that I was broken, but I knew I had to keep it together, or so I thought.

To further complicate things, the woman in Mark 5 likely suffered emotional pain as well. Bound by the rules of her society, she likely carried shame and felt alone. But her story also indicates that somewhere within her she carried hope. Faith was building even in the midst of darkness. She didn't let her desperation turn into despair. She pressed into what she believed in her heart despite the boundaries of her mind, emotions and the rules of her society. She believed that one day she would be healed. If she didn't, why would she bother trying to touch Jesus' robe?

God is Not Responsible for Our Suffering

Let's face it, most of us can relate at some point in our lives to hardship on some level. Unfortunately, trials are part of living in a fallen world and Christians are not immune. Some of us have suffered for a very long time, even on a daily basis. In suffering our minds try to reason with what has happened. Some of us lose perspective and become outraged and deeply disappointed, blaming God for life's circumstances. This is a completely normal response to pain, but the emotions are misplaced. God is not responsible for our suffering.

How do I know this? I had to come to terms with my own issue of blaming God. I believed that He abandoned me in my time of need. I often questioned, how could He let this happen to me? Though I questioned God, desire fueled my search for healing. I'd tried everything else. This time I decided to choose Him and not give up. In my pursuit for God, I set some time aside for studying the Bible. In the quest for knowledge, what I thought about God began to slowly change. God was stirring and shifting me; drawing me closer and replacing my wrong thinking.

Psalm 73:16-17 best describes what I felt during those times.

> *Still, when I tried to figure it out, all I got was a splitting headache ... Until I entered the sanctuary of God. Then I saw the whole picture. MSG*

The sanctuary is the meeting place where God reveals Himself. We've got to go into the sanctuary! You know the saying "How's that working for you?" Trying to figure it out wasn't working too well! I realized that some things in life we never figure out. It was time to take a detour off of this path and it was time to choose to trust Him. It was time to go into the sanctuary.

The sanctuary is also the dwelling place where God meets with His people. Here, there is shelter and protection. He speaks, reveals and revives us. The imagery of Psalm 91:1, 2 best depicts this dwelling place.

> *He who dwells in the shelter of the Most High will abide in the shadow of the Almighty. I will say to the Lord, "My*

refuge and my fortress, my God, in whom I trust!" NASB

The first words of this Scripture immediately indicate that the choice belongs to us. In order to dwell in this shelter, you must first choose to do so. The assertion "I will say" clearly shows that it's available, but we must choose to enter.

The woman could have bought into the belief that God was responsible for her suffering, though there is no evidence of this. Though she suffered, Scripture tells us that her focus was on healing and not what caused her suffering. Her culture was saturated in the Jewish law. But threaded in the culture as well was the hope of a coming Messiah. Malachi 4:2 prophesied:

> But for you who fear My name, the sun of righteousness will
> rise with healing in its wings; and you will go forth and skip
> about like calves from the stall. NASB

Perhaps after hearing rumors of the demoniac being healed (Mark 5:1-20), she thought that she too might receive her chance of healing. No, God wasn't to blame for her suffering. But her faith through suffering was about to lead her to a divine encounter with the Messiah.

Honest to God

Let me give you a word of advice. Always be honest with yourself and with God. You've heard it said, "Honesty is the best policy." I chose to get honest with what I really believed about God.

After sitting and talking to Him regularly, He began to speak to me even more. I closed my mouth and listened. Light began to seep into my dark heart. I felt the warmth of His touch. Healing was occurring and I wanted more!

He showed me how the enemy had led me to believe that I was the only one who felt that God was not there in my time of need. In my wrong thinking, I believed that God caused my suffering because of my sin and that I was unclean.

I believed that my suffering was part of His judgment and that He was punishing me for the things I did and the things that had happened to me in my past. The enemy had me twisted and confused.

As I drew closer to God, He illuminated more of His truth. Ironically, I learned I was not the only one who had thought this way about Him. In the Old Testament, according to Jewish law, it was a common belief that God brought suffering to judge man for sin and disobedience.

"The New Manners and Customs of Bible Times," gives a greater insight about how Jews understood the law.

> *"Jews were promised health if they obeyed God's laws (Exodus 15:26), and they were given a number of health laws (regular rest and relaxation, suitable food, avoidance of contaminated water, marriage regulations, cleanliness, separation from contagious disease), which when followed led to a high level of good health. If the laws were disobeyed, disease resulted (Deuteronomy 28:60-61)."* [2]

If you obeyed God, you reaped the benefit of His blessings. Disobedience resulted in God's judgment. Today many churches still teach and embrace this belief. It also permeates in our culture. The best example of this is found in the book of Job.

The Bible describes Job as a righteous and blameless man who feared God and turned from evil. (Job 1:1) But Job was the poster child for suffering, and his narrative is the model of encouragement for how believers should relate to God in times of suffering. He was honest in expressing what he felt to God.

Job's three friends — who really weren't good friends at all — Eliphaz, Bildad and Zophar came to visit him in his time of distress (Job Chapters 4-31). They believed Job's illness and misfortunes were sent by God as a result of some kind of sin he committed. To correct this, they believed that Job should appeal to God for help.

Job had questions and he wanted answers from God too. He wanted to know what he did to receive this undeserved suffering and where was God in the midst of it all? After Job pours out his heart, God eventually speaks to him; however, not in the manner he had expected. God never answers Job's questions directly. He never receives a full understanding of his suffering, but Job still declares his trust in God and purpose for his life. After losing all of his wealth and family, Job chooses to rest in the mysterious, yet sovereign will of God. He still chose to believe that God is good all the time.

Job's trust in God during the most difficult time of his life challenged me to get honest with myself. I needed to pour out my heart to God like Job did. When I did that, that is when God spoke to me in questions.

He asked, "What do you truly believe about me? And do you believe that I am good?"

After deeply contemplating these questions, I have finally come to a place in my life where I can answer Him honestly.

"Yes! You are a good God all the time!"

I've recognized now that He has always been present in my life, even in the tough times. I don't have a complete understanding of His ways, but I receive more peace as I stay devoted to Him. (For more about suffering, read Deanna's story in Chapter 14.)

Jesus' View on Suffering

In the New Testament, it was a common belief that sin was inherited by your ancestors. This belief was fostered by the Pharisees, a religious sect during that time. They believed that the sins and disobedience of the parents could be passed down to their offspring. The Pharisees were experts at the law, but misunderstood the origin of sin. This belief permeated throughout the culture. This is illustrated in John 9:2-4:

> And His disciples asked Him, "Rabbi, who sinned, this
> man or his parents, that he would be born blind?" Jesus
> answered, "It was neither that this man sinned, nor his
> parents; but it was so that the works of God might be
> displayed in him. We must work the works of Him who sent
> Me as long as it is day; night is coming when no one can
> work. NASB

The blind man suffered from an illness, an illness that during that time would have been commonly believed to have been inherited. Jesus doesn't address the false belief nor does He attribute the man's blindness to his parents. In His view, illness comes from some other source, the activity of the enemy, Satan, and his evil at work in the world.

Jesus also had compassion for those that suffered; he related to them well. This compassion moved Him to hang out with sick and wounded people. He identified with their suffering. You didn't hear Jesus condemning people for their sickness. He was compassionate and it was His compassion that led Him to heal the sick.

We as Christians mustn't feed the lie which attributes that all sickness and hardships are a result of sin, even though sometimes it can be. Other factors like genetics, environment and learned behavior could contribute to these issues. We must also recognize that sickness and hardships often occur simply because we live in a fallen world. But even in this fallen world; there is still hope. We can persevere, and we can overcome our struggles. We are encouraged because Jesus also suffered, yet overcame adversity.

He took on all illness and disease for mankind at the cross. Jesus' passion provides a more complete revelation of suffering. Isaiah 53 depicts Jesus as the Suffering Servant, who was crushed for the sins of the world.

As Christians, we share in the fellowship of His suffering (Philippians 3:10) being shaped and conformed in His image. God never promised that we would live a trial-free life, but He does promise that He'll be with us always. (Psalm 94:14) Until Jesus returns, Christians will endure suffering; but thanks to Jesus, we are never alone.

Job believed that even through his suffering, God is just in a fallen world. This didn't come from an intellectual understanding, but a deep knowing and trust of God and His righteousness. As for me, on the road to healing, my desire to encounter Him accelerated as I sought Him wholeheartedly. Today, I understand that if you truly seek Him with all your heart, you will find Him.

I'm not referring to casual seeking, but willfully choosing to seek after Him and knowing His heart. This requires humility, with the understanding that we are not trying to bribe or manipulate God, but only seek to know Him and love Him.

Anyone Can Approach Jesus

I know what it's like in times of suffering to want to withdraw. Don't do it, no matter how difficult it gets. Be honest with yourself and what you feel. God can handle it. In fact, He already knows. Resist the temptation to shut down and retreat!

Another great lesson we can learn from Job's story is to stay away from bad advice in times of suffering. The enemy is the "accuser of the brethren!" He will use anyone. Like Job, oftentimes the enemy uses people close to us to persuade us that God doesn't love us or that He somehow doesn't care or that He's too busy. In times like these, choose to listen to the Holy Spirit. He is our Helper. Seek wise spiritual counsel from a mature Christian immediately!

Job's dialogue with God taught me that I can boldly approach God. Like the woman in Mark 5, I've learned that He's not afraid of my messy sin. In fact, He extends an invitation to me to rid me from it quickly and permanently.

Scripture indicates that He touched many, but only one was bold enough to touch Him, the fullness of Him, in all His beauty and glory. There are greater implications to this story than the woman's touch, a much more powerful message that needs to be conveyed. It's that Jesus, the Messiah, takes things that are unclean and makes them clean. He will do the same for you!

As for me, I've received a few nuggets of wisdom through all of this. The first, anyone can approach Jesus. He loves us to interact with Him. The second was a reflection I needed to ask myself; is my preoccupation with suffering causing me to miss an opportunity for encounter with God? The answer was, yes. The enemy had me preoccupied with my problems instead of God. This shifted my focus off of Him. For a great portion of my life, my eyes had been fixed on pain and suffering. As I chose to humble myself and receive more healing, I began to understand He gives grace. This grace helps me to understand His heart toward me, drawing me close to Him.

No Pain, No Gain

Looking on Facebook, I noticed that several of my friends had lost weight. Most of their weight loss has not been through dieting, but eating right and exercise. They have disciplined themselves to accomplish their goals. Many have worked hard, getting up as early as 5 a.m. daily. Many that are new to exercise remain faithful to their regimen despite the pain they feel. They know that after a while, the training will still be vigorous, but the pain will slowly subside. They choose to suffer through the pain to get the results they desire.

Through grace, my perspective about Jesus has drastically evolved. He's shown me how He guides, teaches and even disciplines through suffering. How can suffering produce discipline? Suffering is a difficult thing, especially if you have suffered for a long time, but by the grace of God we can connect with Him in suffering.

Our walk with God requires faith, but we must discipline ourselves to stay connected. You may want to set aside a time in your day to sit quietly with God or perhaps read the Word. Through discipline, our relationship with God deepens. When we set up this kind of order in our lives, we create a bond with the Lord that is not easily broken. We become confident in His strength and not our own; therefore, the purpose of discipline isn't to oppress us, but to set us free. We are no longer slaves to these things.

It's only through God's grace that we receive this greater understanding. ,I certainly haven't arrived, but I'm finally on a road, a road to greater discovery about Him. Likewise, the woman in Mark 5 had to deal with pain, but she gained the most important thing — Jesus.

Questions for Thought:

1. We've all had a time where we can say that we've suffered, even if it's for a short period. How did you remain encouraged during that time, and how would you encourage someone else in their time of suffering?

2. The way we view God is important during trying times. Scripture says that He loves and cares for us. Think of a recent time where He showed his love to you either in scripture, nature, through others, a message, hearing His Voice, etc.

3. Many of us can relate to the woman in Mark 5. In what way do you identify with other biblical characters? Look at their strengths. How do these character's strengths encourage you?

4. Did you know that God speaks? Ask God to speak to you about where you are in your healing process. Taking a moment to listen, don't be afraid to respond to what you believe you heard from God.

5. List some ways that you are willing to pursue healing. Examples may be: fasting, finding an accountability partner, studying and meditating on the Word of God, etc.

6. Read the entire chapter of Mark 5. I would like to challenge you to search for the deeper things of God. He will not disappoint. List how Jesus is interacting with each person in the chapter. What does this say about His character?

Prayer:

Lord teach me to be honest about my issues. Help me to open up to you. Help me to understand that suffering can be a way to draw closer to You. Show me a new perspective on Your love for me. Open my ears to hear You more and my eyes to see You more. Give me the strength and peace to enjoy the process. Amen.

— CHAPTER 4 —

The Witness Protection Program

Do you remember the movie, "Did You Hear about the Morgans?" It's a romantic comedy with Hugh Grant and Sara Jessica Parker. The two actors play as a married couple who observe a murder in New York City. Next they are forced to enter into the witness protection program for their safety, given new identities and relocated to a small Wyoming town.

I want to use this movie to illustrate a parallel to the story of the woman. The woman also was removed from her community, lost her identity and was unsafe or at-risk in her environment. I'll elaborate on these themes later in this chapter.

But first let's talk about the U.S. Witness Protection Program. Its purpose is to "provide security, health and safety for government witnesses whose lives are in danger as a result of their testimony against enemies." [3]

The program provides the witness 24-hour protection, a new identity and relocation. In our story in Mark 5, the woman is in an at-risk environment. She has enemies who keep her oppressed and vulnerable. Who were these woman's oppressors?

First, it was her community because she was marginalized as a woman, and not only a woman, but an unclean woman because of Jewish law. Second, she lacked an identity. In that culture she needed a man to validate her. And last, her body was hostile because the sickness worked against her while her emotions kept her oppressed. These unfriendly forces may have caused her to feel alienated or estranged; marginalized as a woman; separated; and ill in her body, mind and emotions.

Focus on Christ, Who Leads Us into Healing Community

The characters in the movie found it extremely difficult to leave a place that they lived all their life. Mr. and Mrs. Morgan had settled into their roles in their careers, families and society. They had settled into a way of life that became part of their identity.

For the woman in Mark 5, she too settled into a way of life in her community. Her identity as a woman was of little influence in her society. Typically, the woman's role was subservient to men. Her duties would have been limited to cooking, cleaning and tending to the needs of the children. At that time, a woman's identity was wrapped in the male leader of the household, father or husband.

Though not clearly stated, the Bible doesn't say if the woman was married or single. If she was married, she wouldn't be able to have sexual relations with her husband because she was considered unclean, reinforcing her lack of identity.

In the same chapter of Mark 5:21-24, we meet Jarius, the leader of the synagogue.

When Jesus had crossed over again in the boat to the other side, a large crowd gathered around Him; and so He stayed by the seashore. 22 One of the synagogue officials named Jairus came up, and on seeing Him, fell at His feet 23 and implored Him earnestly, saying, "My little daughter is at the point of death; please come and lay Your hands on her, so that she will get well and live." 24 And He went off with him; and a large crowd was following Him and pressing in on Him. NASB

Jarius also has an urgent need — he has a sick daughter. As a father, Jarius was allowed to approach Jesus because the young girl's identity was established through him. This was an acceptable part of the culture during this time. But the unnamed woman had no male to represent her. She was solely identified through her suffering.

Today women can do and be anything they choose. But many women still struggle with identity issues. Some women marry a man to make them feel complete. I know, I was one of them. I lacked an identity and I thought marriage would complete me. While it is true that marriage is a beautiful union between a man and a woman, if you are marrying a man to complete yourself, then you'll likely be disappointed.

I can't tell you how many ladies that I know who claim to have found or are looking for their "knight in shining armor." After a few years they find that the armor isn't quite as shiny. It becomes dull. The lackluster in appearance is because all of the woman's identity is poured into the man, a man with limited resources for a deeply wounded woman.

Jaimee and I met in the St. Joseph County jail while we were ministering to incarcerated women. We both agree that one of the biggest prayer requests we heard was, "Will you pray for my man?" While yes, they wanted out of jail, their minds constantly defaulted to their "man."

I would think, "Why? This man beat you, he's left you; in fact, he's the reason you're here."

Then Jaimee and I would be out with our girlfriends and realized their stories sounded similar to the women in the jail. So we saw that this is a bigger issue with women in general. It kind of got us to thinking, why are we as women so wrapped up in a man?

Through deep discussion, we feel that it all boils down to love. These women, like us, just want to be loved. Why? Because that is one of the reasons we were created — to love and be loved.

So how do we eventually get into an unhealthy relationship where we use a man as a means to fill us?

I believe many of these issues start at a very young age. Somewhere there is a void that was created that never got fulfilled. This empty place cries out in agony to be filled with something. Until health comes to this place, the pain will persist. We try to fill it with whatever we can — designer clothing, big houses, shallow friendships, partying — and sometimes we use a man. But Jesus fills voids! He knows how to complete those areas that we are lacking in; it's His specialty. First, we must believe He can and is willing to do it, thean we wait for Him and be patient in our process. Waiting isn't just twiddling your thumbs aimlessly; waiting involves an expectancy that we will one day be made whole. When Jesus ministers health, our security and identity does come from a man.

In our focus on Christ, we cannot forget about community. If you are in a healthy community, you will have healthy relationships to model from. In the movie mentioned earlier, the Morgans are ready to divorce, but they are forced to live in a small town with another couple. This other couple showcases a healthy relationship. The Morgans can see that this couple has something they don't; however, the Morgans need to make the choice to change.

Change is not easy, but in some cases it's necessary. Women who have their focus on a man to fulfill them need to redirect their focus toward Christ and find a healthy community where they can grow, mature and flourish. This is the job of the church body, to display a healthy community of believers who encourage, pray and share life together in Christ.

Then when you meet your "man," you won't need things from him that he wasn't created to give you in the first place. A man does not complete you and was not intended to be your identity.

My husband married a woman with lots of baggage. I didn't go into our marriage for the sole purpose of Cary fixing me, but the longer we were married the more I looked to him to make me feel better. I struggled with my identity because of my upbringing. Cary had always helped to strengthen me during difficult times and that was great, but after a while I became frustrated and disappointed with him. Recently, I got a revelation. God showed me that my emotional pain was way too deep and it was never Cary's job to heal me or fill the void in my heart.

Jesus, on the other hand, was happy to take the job if I was truly willing to give Him a chance. Cary was happy for Him to step in. Jesus wants my identity to be wrapped in Him. Jesus has the job of strengthening and fixing me. That means Cary is off the hook!

I also realized for myself that I needed to be a part of a healthy community. So my husband and I started a Friday night fellowship in our home. I think of it this way in the imagery of the cross. I have a vertical relationship with Christ, meaning my gaze is toward Him. But it's also important to have a horizontal relationship where I have to look side to side to engage other brother and sisters. Jesus taught there are two great commandments; love God and love your neighbor.

> 'And you shall love the Lord your God with all your heart, and with all your soul,, and will your soul, and with all your mind, and with all your strength' The second is this, 'You shall love your neighbor as yourself.' There is no other commandment greater than these. Mark 12:30-31 NASB

Establishing a New Identity

Establishing a new identity can be both exciting and uncomfortable. You know that it's necessary, but you don't have a grid for it yet, because it's new. As you continue to navigate through this new identity, tension can build, putting you in a position to have to choose between letting old habits die and accepting healthier new ones. When a person enters into the Witness Protection Program, they assume a new identity. Their old identity is wiped away and they receive documentation validating their new life. Jesus established a new identity for this woman in Mark 5. After the woman makes a desperate move to boldly touch Jesus' fringe, He rescues her from her identity crisis. Her faith in Him has moved her out of a false identity into her new one. How does Jesus do this?

First, after the woman touches his fringe, He responds to her touch by saying, "Who touched me?" The woman, knowing that she wasn't permitted to touch Jesus based on her social status and her unclean state, had desperately and inconspicuously touched His fringe. Jesus acknowledges her because there is something different about her touch. She touched more than a piece of cloth, she touched the transforming power of Jesus!

Remember, there were many people in the crowd that were pressing against Him. In fact, the disciples were shocked when Jesus asked the question, "Who touched Me?" I can hear them saying. "Seriously Jesus, you have all these people pressing against You and You ask who?" But there was indeed something about her touch that moved Jesus. I believe that if you are pressing into Jesus with all you have, you are always going to get MORE than what you are asking for!

Something happens when you come to God in faith. We are changed and He stands up and takes notice. It's not that Jesus was unaware of the woman's touch, but it was indeed her faith that caused Him to take notice.

I am convinced that there's a difference between brushing against Jesus and those who truly touch Him. A brush for some may be enough to get healing, but touching Him is transforming.

When I first started this journey, my desire was for healing, but as I drew closer to Him, my passion was for transformation. I wanted the heart change and the mind renewal and every other benefit that came through fellowship with Him.

In the woman's story, there were many other needy people who touched Jesus, but only one encounter actually caught His attention. As for me, I do not wish to live in a place of constant need and pity. I choose to live in my new identity; a place where, Paul says, Christ's strength is made perfect in our weakness; therefore we have permission to boast in our weakness. (2 Corinthians 12:9)

In the woman's case, she was weak in her body and lacked in other areas of her life, but when she touched Christ, the weakness went away. Therefore, she could happily claim that Christ made her strong. She had nothing but God's strength.

Paul found this place of confidence in his new identity in Christ.

Establishing your new identity doesn't require striving, but it does require believing in Jesus. There is no other way to put it. You must have desire and you must believe. No one can do it for you. You can have every person you know praying and believing for you. Don't get me wrong. That's a good thing, but until you choose to step out and reach for Jesus, you stay in a survival mode trapped in a false identity.

Don't be afraid to reach out and touch Him. Think of it this way, everything we need is just an arm's reach away. In reality, He is closer to you than you think.

After the woman touches Jesus' fringe, He not only publicly acknowledges the woman but He calls her "daughter." This was no small thing! This one word publicly affirms her, establishing a new identity. Remember the woman had no male representative. Jesus invites her into His family. Nowhere in the New Testament does He call another woman, "daughter."

She has entered into Jesus' Witness Protection Program. She is a witness for Him and her story has changed. She receives ongoing protection, 24/7. She is safe. She has been adopted; she has a Father and she's also a part of another Kingdom — God's Kingdom. Only Jesus has the true authority to declare her acceptance and validation of a new life.

Lastly, Jesus tells the woman, "Your faith has made you whole" and to "Go in peace!" The word *whole* comes from the Greek word *sozo*, which encompasses not only healing to her body, but her mind, soul and spirit as well. In other words, the woman's faith in Jesus caused her to receive not only healing, but eternal life; a new identity. Her touch and His words freed the woman. She is no longer bound by the identity that kept her in hiding for years.

I'd like to encourage you that regardless of where you are in your process, you can be used by God. Our witness is vital. Indeed, I can't deny that it's great to have a testimony that you're healed, but it's also powerful to have a testimony that you are standing! I'm one of those still standing, and I'm confident of God's purpose in my life!

The Importance of Community

Growing up, my family and I always enjoyed visits to my Uncle John and Aunt Marguerite's home on the weekends. We played games, ate together, talked and laughed. I loved hanging out with my cousins, dancing together doing the "Soul Train" line. These were some of the happiest times, sharing life with family at my aunt and uncle's house. We had great fellowship in their home. From my perspective, in my little world, this was true community.

In the early church, believers fellowshipped in each other's homes. Acts 2:44-47 provides us with some perspective on the way community functioned then. It says they broke bread at each other's homes and shared everything they had. They had a common union through God's Spirit. "Merrian-Webster's Dictionary" describes community as "a unified body of individuals; people of common interest living in a particular area."[4]

Community gatherings in the Old and New Testaments were a vital aspect of the Jewish people, especially in the synagogue on the Sabbath. Prior to Jesus, the priests were mediators between the people and God. They offered sacrifices for the sins of the community. Because of Jesus, we no longer need a mediator. Hebrews 3:1 identifies Jesus as the High Priest. We have been granted direct access to Him. We are free to approach Him to touch and taste of His goodness.

"When Solomon's Temple had been destroyed and the Jews were in exile, they survived by gathering together on the Sabbath to learn about their law and traditions. The word *synagogue* literally means gathering-together-places."[5]

Community is relational. We as human beings cry out for relationship. It's part of our nature. We were created by God for relationship with Him and others. The Bible uses words like adoption (Ephesians 1:5), fellowship (1 John. 1:3), love (John. 3:16), etc. to describe His affection toward His people and our relationship toward each other.

In today's society, technology presents an obstacle for our deep need for fellowship. Social media, video conferencing, texting and email have caused us to distance ourselves and challenge our need for intimacy. In my humble opinion, nothing expresses how much you care about a person more than face to face communication. I regularly try to do a girl's night out with friends. My husband and I have regular date nights and frequently get together with friends in our home to stay connected.

We, as the body of Christ, must stay connected. Can you imagine if God's only means of communication to us was through an email or text? That sounds ridiculous! Then why is it OK for us? Relationship is God's design. There is purpose in it. In Genesis, God said that it was not good for His first human creation, Adam, to be alone, nor is it good for His people.

A Community Parable

In Mark 5:1-20, Jesus encounters a man that is possessed by many demons who was alienated from his community, living in the tombs. He was considered unclean and required isolation, an exile (Mark 5:5). Jesus casts out the man's demons and restores him back to his community. Jesus healed the man not only for the purpose of performing a miracle in the man's life, even though that was very important. Jesus was equally concerned about the man's social standing in his community. In short, the man needed to be healed, but he also needed a place where he could have fellowship with others.

The demoniac man, the woman with the issue of blood and Jarius' daughter are all considered unclean according to the law. This theme runs through Mark 5, the woman gets healed by faith and gets sent back into the community. The little girl is healed and is sent back into the community. Jesus not only heals, but he reveals the greater plan. These are individuals who become living testimonies of the power of Jesus in their lives.

I'm Accepted in His Community

Lack of acceptance is one of the greatest threats to a community, especially a Christian community. I learned this lesson through my own personal experience. In 1988, I chose to give my life to Jesus. Right after that, He placed me in a great Christian fellowship with outstanding teachers. The group consisted of mostly college students from a variety of cities and church backgrounds. There was a mixture of students that grew up in the church and others that were new to the faith.

As you can imagine in an environment like this, the atmosphere was charged with lots of energy and questions. The leadership provided foundational teaching centered on how to live in our new identity in Christ.

But there was also a lack of maturity among the students that didn't foster an environment for wounded new believers like me. I perceived myself as a social outcast. I wasn't what some call, "churched," meaning I didn't speak church lingo and was unfamiliar with church tradition. This sometimes made me feel alienated by the "churched" clique.

I was talked about because of the way I dressed. I didn't know what to wear to church; I just wanted to be there. My lack of knowledge of simple biblical principles caused glares and snickers in our Friday night Bible studies. This was a whole new experience for me. I thought I was supposed to be a new creation, but I guess some didn't get the memo.

Despite some of the small personality issues, God did bless me with many good friends back then. Many of them are close to me even today.

Recently, I received a phone call from one of those friends that I highly respect. This person called to congratulate me on the recent success of speaking at my very first conference.

During that conversation, the person told me about an incident that happened 20 years ago that I was unaware of. We had traveled to another ministrya., with a group of students from our ministry to be baptized.

Someone in the group asked, "How could God baptize someone so unclean?"

My friend told me that they were referring to me. I was devastated! Why would my friend tell me this now? This happened 20 years ago. My friend explained that she was encouraged and amazed at how God transformed the pain of my past for ministry today. After she told me this, for the first time in my life, I realized that the work Jesus had been doing on the inside was finally bearing fruit.

I had to stop to briefly ponder the same question, "How could God baptize someone so unclean?"

At that point it hit me, this is why He suffered. He suffered for me! His sacrifice makes me clean. The blood He shed makes me clean! That's why He can baptize me. I don't have to search anymore for acceptance. I am accepted in His community. It doesn't matter how dirty I am or how dirty you are, His blood makes us clean.

What Community Meant for the Woman in Mark 5

The woman in Mark 5 was subject to the Jewish law, which states:

> When a woman has a discharge, if her discharge in her body is blood, she shall continue in her menstrual impurity for seven days; and whoever touches her shall be unclean until evening. [20] Everything also on which she lies during her menstrual impurity shall be unclean, and everything on which she sits shall be unclean. Leviticus 15:19, 20 NASB

During this time, anything that her blood touched would be rendered ritually unclean. So if she bled through her clothes and someone touched her blood, they would be unclean until evening.

The Bible doesn't display her state of mind, but (Was she really not allowed to worship?) it's possible she may have removed herself from her place of worship, not wanting to put others at risk. If this is true, the woman is alienated once again. And that would compound an already complex issue, her inability to receive support from the church for spiritual connection. It's important to note, however, that even though the woman was considered ritually unclean, she was not sinful.

Faith requires that we step out of something that we become familiar with and step into a place of trust; a total trust in Jesus. It means that you may have to do something or some things that you haven't done before or even revisiting a place that was too difficult in the past with a new perspective. Don't be afraid to go there!

Like the woman, you may have to crawl or humble yourself to get there, and it may seem like you are alone or that a giant is in your way. Remember that faith in Jesus will be your greatest assurance to victory. When she made up her mind to step out of fear and step into faith, she placed herself on the road toward healing. Her faith healed her body, mind and soul and she was restored back to her community. Her faith yielded far more results than what she had originally asked for.

Questions for Thought

Identity

1. Who do you believe you are? Do you behave like you are a child of God despite your circumstances?

2. Has your identity ever been wrapped up in your possessions, job title, husband, children, etc.? Ask the Lord if your identity is solely in Him? If not, ask Him to bring you deeper into your identity in Him.

3. Because of the woman's faith, she enters into a new community with a new identity. Colossians 3:10-11 encourages us to "put on the new self." Here Paul makes no distinction between Greek or Jew, circumcised or uncircumcised, male or female. All who believe in Christ by faith are saved and are citizens of heaven with a new identity. What does it mean to you to put on your new self?

Community

4. How important is the body of believers to you in your walk with Christ?

5. Are you involved with a body of believers in a small group, bible study, discipleship or church? Why or why not?

6. Through your experience in healing, what do you have to offer the church body to make it a better place?

Prayer

Lord help me to see who I am in You; that my identity is in You, not my man, not my job and not my possessions. Take me deeper into the things of You. Reveal to me my weakness so I can boast in Your strength alone. Show me what it's like to partake in the truest sense of community. Let me be someone who accepts others right where they are at like You have accepted me. Amen.

— CHAPTER 5 —

Restoration

About six months ago, Jaimee and her husband's family spent a week putting the finishing touches on remodeling and decorating her and Nathan's bedroom. I came over for a crab boil one of the nights, and when I walked into the house, the whole downstairs was full of stuff: pillows, pictures, knick knacks, basically everything that was going to eventually go upstairs. She had this flowered cream vase that her mother-in-law had purchased, and it was elegant. Unfortunately, with all the traffic and clutter, the vase fell off the kitchen table and the neck of it broke into about 20 small pieces.

Jaimee was bummed because she loved that vase and there was no way to purchase another one. So she decided she was going to put this vase back together piece by piece. She spent the evening with glue and started the puzzle. By morning it was back together and dry, though you could still see the cracks on the outside. That was not good enough for Jaimee, so still determined, she tied a ribbon around the neck of the vase, making it look like new.

Recently, I was at the house to see the newly finished upstairs, and Jaimee showed me the vase. I couldn't tell that it had ever been broken, until she showed me what was behind the ribbon. It was now noticeable. Then she showed me the inside of the vase, which looked worse than the outside. I could see every crack on the inside, but it sure was masked from the outside.

This vase could be seen as a metaphor for our own brokenness. On the outside, everything looks OK, but on the inside — not so much. A lot of times as women, we tend to hide our cracks because we have not come into the full understanding of who God is or we are afraid to give ourselves to Him in total trust. So we mask our pain. We put on something pretty, and no one knows what is underneath.

Just like that beautiful vase needed to be carefully put back together from its broken state, likewise we need restoration.

The Three-Part Process

I see restoration as being a three-part process. The first part occurs when we give our lives to the Lord. When this happens, there is a heart change. We invite Jesus to come in and abide in our hearts. The Bible refers to this as salvation. Salvation in itself brings about healing and restoration because our sins are forgiven and our hearts are restored back to God.

> It wasn't so long ago that we ourselves were stupid and stubborn, dupes of sin, ordered every which way by our glands, going around with a chip on our shoulder, hated and hating back. But when God, our kind and loving Savior God, stepped in, he saved us from all that. It was all his doing; we had nothing to do with it. He gave us a good bath, and we came out of it new people, washed inside and out by the Holy Spirit. Our Savior Jesus poured out new life so generously. God's gift has restored our relationship with Him and given us back our lives. And there's more life to come — an eternity of life! You can count on this. Titus 3:3-8 MSG

> Because of this decision we don't evaluate people by what they have or how they look. We looked at the Messiah that way once and got it all wrong, as you know. We certainly don't look at Him that way anymore. Now we look inside, and what we see is that anyone united with the Messiah gets a fresh start, is created new. The old life is gone; a new life burgeons! Look at it! All this comes from the God who settled the relationship between us and Him, and then called us to settle our relationships with each other. God put the world square with Himself through the Messiah, giving the world a fresh start by offering forgiveness of sins. God has given us the task of telling everyone what He is doing. We're Christ's representatives. God uses us to persuade men and women to drop their differences and enter into God's work of making things right between them. We're speaking for Christ Himself now: Become friends with God; He's

already a friend with you. 2 Corinthians 5:16-20 MSG

The second part of this process comes as we mature in our walk with the Lord. We are restored by choosing to have our minds renewed, or in the simplest sense, focusing on Christ and the scriptures. We also walk in the power of God through the inner workings of the Holy Spirit (2 Corinthians 3:18). I believe this part of our walk of faith can be testing to most believers because it challenges us to go deeper. But scripture encourages us to work out our salvation with fear and trembling (Philippians 2:12).

The power of His love has the ability to heal and restore. I know this for my own life because I am in this second process of restoration. In it, I am growing and maturing in my walk with God. Day by day, I have to make a conscious effort to choose to let God help me with my thoughts. The process requires an ongoing deliberateness and sometimes even discipline to choose to set my mind on the truth. This steadfast diligence pays off when I see how much the process has made me stronger and wiser.

I can also say that many memories of abuse are no longer tormenting me.

I used to have difficulty being around certain family members because it would trigger memories of abuse. I had to avoid movies that had themes of abuse. Familiar scents and music took me back to a place of fear, anger and pain.

Now I can look at these memories and there is an absence of fear, anger and pain; it's been replaced with peace.

So the way I see it, when God heals, He replaces your pain for peace, joy, love, etc. When you receive those things a powerful transformation happens in your soul (body, mind and emotions) that feeds hope. Then faith increases and it's like putting fuel on a fire. Something gets ignited in you to believe for more. That's what keeps me pursing wholeness.

I want to make it clear, though, that the absence of pain does not necessarily mean there is true peace. You can go through a difficult situation and think that you have been healed, because your emotions are not stirred up. And perhaps you have received a measure of peace, but what I have found in my process is that true peace comes when there is an expression of the fruit of the Spirit that flows out of your life. You don't struggle anymore.

The third part is a future event that will happen when Jesus returns to gather His people. This is the ultimate part of our restoration that is where we will suffer no more sorrow and pain. In this place, we will abide and reign with Christ Jesus.

Jaimee restored the vase back to what it looked like originally, but it had imperfections. These are the limitations we have as humans to fix our own brokenness. When Jesus returns, there will be no imperfections. Our identity is restored and we live in a perfect community. In essence, we will live in heaven and all of its fullness. No longer will we have to hide or be ashamed about our imperfections. There will be no need to disguise our cracks and brokenness; we won't need it, we'll be perfect inside and outside.

This is what part three looks like — process number two is over! For me, there will be no more mental torment, depression or anxiety. I believe there will be no more of these memories. I will know fully what joy is. There is joy in every memory on earth. I believe I can have it here on earth, but if I don't, it's still going to happen in eternity.

> *They will hunger no longer, nor thirst anymore; nor will the sun beat down on them, nor any heat; for the Lamb in the center of the throne will be their shepherd, and will guide them to springs of the water of life; and God will wipe every tear from their eyes. Revelation 7:16, 17 NASB*

> *And I heard a loud voice from the throne, saying, "Behold, the tabernacle of God is among men, and He will dwell among them, and they shall be His people, and God Himself will be among them, and He will wipe away every tear from their eyes; and there will no longer be any death; there will no longer be any mourning, or crying, or pain; the first things have passed away." Revelation 21:3, 4 NASB*

The Journey with Jesus

God continues to constantly pursue His people. His desire is for humanity to be restored back to Him. If you read the Bible you will find God persistently and gently wooing His people to Him. It's the ultimate love story, filled with emotion and hope for reunion. He is passionate about His people and desires to have relationship with us.

For this reason God sent Jesus, His only Son. Jesus was without sin but chose to suffer, bleed and die for the sins of the world. Through His life, death and resurrection, we can enter into a relationship with God. We have access to Him. He paid the price for us so that we experience God intimately and live a life of victory and freedom ... now that's love!

I'd love to tell you that I've received 100 percent healing from my issues. But, as I mentioned earlier, I need to be honest with you; I'm still in process, as we all are. There's no shame in admitting this because I know that God is faithful, and in life sometimes we must learn to rejoice in our baby steps. I've also learned that He will use the sum of all the things that happen in our lives to draw us close to Him — even our struggles. Scripture tells us that we can be confident is this:

> *And we know that God causes all things to work together*
> *for good to those who love God, to those who are called*
> *according to His purpose. Romans 8:28. NASB*

Today, He is using my voice to speak life, truth and destiny to those who don't know they have one. The message is about God's amazing love and His healing power. To me, getting what I want in healing is becoming less important than discovering His love and truth. This is what happened to the woman in Mark 5. She was restored to wholeness and was placed in a position where she had a voice to share with her community what Jesus had done, all because she stepped out in faith. Her single-mindedness caused her to courageously pursue healing through Jesus.

These past two years have opened doors for me like never before. God has divinely put me in places where I would never dream I'd be in my lifetime. He has put me in several places of influence, but most importantly, He has allowed me to serve in my community.

I know for certain that God is doing this because I've been pursuing healing. He wants to use me to tell others about the power of His healing even while I'm still in process. I would like to make it clear, however, that what God is doing in my life is not about works or even how well I can behave. Unlike with fellow human beings, I no longer have to perform to receive His approval.

In fact, I'm not really sure that I understand it all completely. One thing that I am convinced about is that my faith is playing an important part in my journey toward restoration. If I'm willing to give Him everything, He will fill my place of emptiness.

As I've stated before, the woman in our story did receive a full healing, but that wasn't the point of the story. The point was she too had to go through a process that led her on a faith journey to Jesus. I'm sure there were many times she wanted to give up, leave the faith, hide and maybe even die. Even on the day that she went to touch Jesus, there were probably many obstacles against her, but she pressed through and Jesus met her. He will meet you, too, because for as much as we are desperate for Him, He desires us more and wants the wholeness for us even more than we do.

Forgiveness Restores Justice

Another very important lesson that I've learned on my journey is the importance of forgiveness. Unforgiveness disrupts relationships — both our relationship with God and others. Forgiveness is not only designed for the removal of sin. It's also an important part of the process of restoration. Forgiveness reunites the relationship with the person that hurt us and with God.

At one point in my life I wanted justice for all the things that happened to me and those that hurt me. I was seeking revenge for the pain in my heart. Today I have a different perspective. I see things through new lenses. The justice I sought was harmful and destructive. Jesus judges righteously. As I continue to walk and grow in the Lord, I begin to see things the way He sees things with righteous lenses.

As I walk through this process of restoration, I see fruit from my suffering. To be honest, though, I still struggle, but I wouldn't change a thing about my life. I know that may be hard for many to hear, but it's true. When I look at how the pain of my past has plunged me into a passionate hunger for Jesus, all of the hurts and pains from my past get smaller and smaller. Like the Apostle Paul, I'm starting to get excited when God shows me where I'm wounded. I can then confidently give it to Him and use it as an opportunity to get closer to Him. (2 Corinthians 12:9)

This pursuit has strengthened my love for Him. As God pours out His love on me, I've found that it begins to pour out of me. I'm able to love because of His love for me, even those who have hurt me in the past. The power of His love gives me the freedom to forgive; I no longer seek justice for myself, but now I seek His righteousness. Love sets you and the person you have held captive free forever.

> Be even-tempered, content with second place, quick to forgive an offense. Forgive as quickly and completely as the Master forgave you. Colossians 3:13 MSG

You've heard both my story and the woman's story in Mark 5, but without Jesus we have no story. In the beginning, I thought my testimony was only about my process of healing, but as I stated earlier, I see things with a new perspective, more clearly, with the eyes of one who is being restored day by day.

My new sight helps my focus. Just like a new pair of glasses, what was once blurry is now coming into focus. I can forgive and release everyone who has hurt me, because my vision has cleared and He has my gaze!

That's one of the reasons why I believe my suffering at one point was prolonged. It's hard to find God in the darkness of my mind. Unbelief and wrong thinking kept me blind and incapable of seeing His work in my life. I had no vision and the enemy was happy to keep me blind. Jesus has always been there for me, but I only saw the enemy and chose to listen to him.

I get it now. The process has moved my gaze off of my issues and on to the Holy One. I've been telling people for so long about what the enemy has done to me. That used to be the center of a lot of my conversations; the devil did this, and the devil did that.

I'm done with talking about the devil. Jesus wants His story told. He wants me to share what He has done in my life. He was drawing me to Him even during my time of suffering. He wants me to see Him for who He really is! Restoration is payback for the devil.

In our stories, the woman and I are merely props on the much larger stage and Jesus plays the lead role. We must remember that our stories aren't centered on us, but how He overcame so that we may, too, overcome.

The kind of justice that brings healing was served in the life, death and resurrection of Jesus. As for me, I don't feel like anyone needs to pay me back and I don't need to get revenge. The victory over my past has given me the confidence to help others fight for their futures. That's the true power of Jesus. Restoration makes you feel like LIFE IS WORTH LIVING AGAIN.

Share Your Story

I was walking on the campus of the University of Notre Dame recently and I met a woman. In conversation, I started telling her about this book. She eagerly shared her story as a cancer survivor.

Fourteen years ago she went through breast cancer. She did chemotherapy and lost her hair. Through it all she had a confidence that the Lord was with her and she was going to overcome this disease. To this day, she still feels honored and blessed to be alive. So she gives back to other cancer patients. No matter where she is, the Lord leads who to others who are sick. Then she goes up to that person and asks them about it. She says she has never been wrong. Then she gives the person a hug, prays for them and encourages them by sharing her story of healing.

One of the biggest benefits to living a redeemed life is that God gives you a testimony. After the woman touched the hem of Jesus' garment she was healed, but something else happens — she was reconciled back to her community and Jesus wanted everyone to know. In the presence of all her people, He asked the woman to share with them her story. In doing this, the woman, for the first time in her life, had a voice.

Her faith in Jesus gives her a voice; she is a carrier of good news. Restoration gives the once nameless woman an identity. Jesus now refers to her by her new name, "Daughter." She is the daughter of the King.

In the history of the church, women have been pummeled by a male dominated institution that, in many cases, erroneously utilized the Word of God to keep women ignorant and oppressed. In spite of this injustice, God has continued to use women throughout history to fulfill His purpose in the world.

He gave His first hint of this by commissioning Mary Magdalene, who was the first evangelist, to proclaim the good news of the resurrection to the 11 disciples who were hiding in the upper room in fear of persecution. (Luke 24:10). The good news predicates on the acceptance of the witness of Mary, a woman. As the church developed and progressed, God patiently and strategically used women to reveal Himself to His people.

Today the Lord has given nearly 40 women a platform to write for this book. They have a voice! They freely share their stories of brokenness and restoration through Jesus. Some have received a full healing in their area of struggle, while others have received some healing and are diligent in their pursuit for more. Since Jaimee and I have started this project, several women have shared with us that they have received opportunities to minister and share their stories in different venues. Through faith, God has blessed them with more healing.

We all have stories. Every believer should be able to point to a time in their lives where they encountered Jesus. That's part of the salvation experience. Your story may not have the drama of the woman in Mark 5, but we all have a story. Many find it difficult to share their testimony because they don't feel their story is relevant. They believe that if they don't have a powerful transforming experience, then their testimony is disqualified. That's the furthest thing from the truth.

If you long for others to know God's love and truth, share your testimony. The purpose of your testimony is to share the message of Jesus through what He has done in your life. By doing so, it opens up an invitation for that person or people you are sharing with to step in and believe by faith that God can and will do the same thing for them. We are saved and redeemed by the transforming power of the Gospel. The pressure of how good our stories sound to others is not as important as the message of the Gospel itself. The good news is the central theme of a testimony. Don't be afraid to share your story!

In Summary

Whatever you are going through, you are not alone. About 2,000 years ago, a nameless woman was suffering in her body, lacked an identity and was estranged from her community. She was desperate and she believed that Jesus could heal her. She went for it. She pressed through all the obstacles. She touched Jesus and He gave her more than she could imagine. She was made whole in her body, received an identity as a daughter, and was restored back into her community. She was made whole.

Don't feed into the lie that that was then and this is now. God is the same yesterday, today and tomorrow. He doesn't favor one of us more than the other. What He does for one, He can and will do for you.

In part two of this book, you will read testimonies of women just like you. You may not be able to relate to all their stories, but you will be encouraged by the power of God working in each and every one of these woman's lives. Each woman's story and process is different, but I believe it's always about going deeper in our relationship with God and letting His glory shine through us.

> *And they overcame him because of the blood of the Lamb and because of the word of their testimony. Revelation 12:11 NASB*

Questions for Thought

1. Where have you seen healing in your life?

2. If restoration and healing are a process, what might this mean for how we build expectations for God and the community of God's people?

3. In what ways do you think Jesus' life, death and resurrection are effective to bring about your restoration and healing?

4. In what ways do you feel you've experienced injustice? How does the story of the woman in Mark 5 and the story of Jesus more broadly help you think about what it would mean to receive justice?

5. What women do you know who have inspiring testimonies? And what makes their testimonies inspiring?

6. What is your testimony of healing? If you're not healed completely, what is your testimony so far? Write it out, return to it when you need to remember what the Lord has done for you.

Prayer

Lord thank you for dying on the cross and shedding Your blood so that I could be restored to You. Show me where I still need restoration in my life. If I have a wrong mindset about You or my situation, show me so I can have a new perspective. Lord I trust You and believe that You want to make me whole in my body, mind and emotions. Show me the next steps in becoming whole. No matter how hard it is, I won't give up. I will keep seeking after You, removing my focus on my circumstance. Amen.

PART 2

The Women's Stories

— CHAPTER 6 —

Surrender Heals Broken Marriage

BY MICLE

I have a beautiful life. Some might call it "charmed." Others would opt for "blessed." Ray and I both have good jobs, we have a beautiful home and we're part of a fabulous church.

It wasn't always so wonderful. I did my best to mess it up, but God put it back together. Then, my husband did his best to mess it up. But God. But God …

This isn't an easy story to tell. It's not pretty. But the devil is having a field day with marriages today, and because of what God has done, I have to stand up and say that it does *not* have to be this way. There is forgiveness. There is reconciliation. There is restoration. There is hope. There is *always* hope. Remember, love — real love, Godly love — hopes all things (1 Corinthians 13).

***

Ray and I met when I was 14. Yep, 14. We were engaged by the time I was 17, and married when I was 18. Looking back, I realize I was just a kid. I had no business getting married that young. I had no idea what was going on. I knew nothing about life and the real world. But, no one could tell me that then. I was on top of the world, in love, and no one was going to stop me from getting what I wanted.

Three years in, I was almost done with college. Ray had worked hard to make sure the bills got paid and we didn't go on food stamps. In fact, we already had our first little house. But I felt empty. Dissatisfied. Ray was working nights, while I went to school and worked in the day-time. During the hours we were actually awake at the same time, Ray did his thing, and I did mine. Gradually, I grew to resent him. The only time he showed any interest in me, it seemed, was when he had "ulterior motives."

Meanwhile, someone at work began to pay attention to me. A lot of attention. And I liked it. He made me promises. He told me I was pretty. He told me he liked the way I smelled. Ray never said those things.

Eventually, Ray found out what was happening. It broke him in a way that I didn't know anyone could be broken. I remember the look on his face. It still grieves me to think about how I had crushed him. In that moment, as I looked into his face — stricken, drawn, broken — I decided that if Ray ever stumbled, I would forgive him. After all, if I could do something so terrible so easily, how could I ever judge him for doing the same?

Shortly thereafter, we sold our home and moved to the Dallas area. I went to work for a Fortune 500 company, and Ray went to work for a specialty hospital, doing work that he loved and was passionate about, but he was still working nights. We found a church where we got connected, and began helping with the youth group. Things were much better, it seemed. We were back on track.

Sometime during the next couple of years, God gave me a vision. I don't remember where I was when it happened, but I can still see it now just as clearly as I could then. I was sitting on our bed, with my back against the headboard, my knees drawn to my chest. The bedroom was ours, but it had been decorated differently. The emotion that struck me was brokenness, grief and utter isolation. Super-imposed over our three-dimensional bedroom was a huge being, standing behind the bed, with his wings stretched all the way over the bed, wingtips coming together just over the footboard. At that time, I hadn't ever read Psalms 91:

> *Whoever dwells in the shelter of the Most High will rest in the shadow of the Almighty. I will say of the LORD, "He is my refuge and my fortress, my God, in whom I trust." Surely he will save you from the fowler's snare and from the deadly pestilence. He will cover you with his feathers, and under his wings you will find refuge; his faithfulness will be your shield and rampart. You will not fear the terror of night, nor the arrow that flies by day, nor the pestilence that stalks in the darkness, nor the plague that destroys at midday. Psalms 91:1-6 NIV*

Things were going so well, the vision confused me. We were happy, I thought. I was always with people, busy doing stuff, and I couldn't fathom how I could ever be so forlorn, so completely alone. For a time, I forgot about it completely, until 2004, the year of our 10th anniversary. Then, as my world came crashing down, I suddenly realized how such devastation was possible.

Ray confessed to having an affair with a woman who was his carpool partner. I immediately forgave him, told him I understood and asked if he would be willing to work on things. He thought about it for a few days, and agreed. I immediately set out to make his life as perfect as I could, planning romantic weekends, clever dates and whatever else I thought might rekindle our fire. I thought we were headed in the right direction, when I received a phone call from the husband of the "other woman."

Mr. Other Woman had hidden a miniature tape recorder in her car, which picked up a conversation between her and Ray, about how wonderful their "encounter" that morning had been. On the day in question, I knew he had been home, because he had made a big deal about having washed the sheets. Ouch.

I called him at work, and asked if he had something he wanted to tell me. He dodged the question, and tried not to answer. I told him that if he didn't come clean with me right then, I was coming to the hospital and we would get it all out in the open, in front of God and everybody. He switched phones.

That night was the most painful night of my existence. After having poured myself out for him, doing everything I could think of to lure his affections, he was still cheating — and lying about it. I stripped the sheets and the comforter off the bed and threw them in the driveway. I considered driving to the hospital and letting the air out of all her tires. I debated slashing the mattress. My heart was so broken, it was difficult to even catch my breath. The next few weeks, I walked through my life, like a ghost, a shell of the person I once was. Then I remembered the vision.

God had shown me that despite my brokenness, and how lonely I felt, He was with me. He knew this day was coming, and He loved me so much, that He had done something to help me get through it. Even though it wasn't His plan, He had seen the beginning from the end. This assurance gave me the resolve I needed to face lawyers, Ray and the possibility of a future without him. It enabled me to surrender my marriage to God. I realized that the outcome was completely out of my hands. I had done everything I could. The rest was up to God, and how Ray responded to Him.

Ironically, this act of surrender was what brought Ray home. I stopped hounding him with hysterical phone calls. I stopped obsessing about him, embracing the peace of God instead.

Later, Ray told me that his wake-up call came after our meeting with my attorney. As we were leaving, he told me that if I ever needed anything, I could always call him. Calmly, I responded, "It's not your job to take care of me anymore." It was God's. Ray said that when he heard those words, he instantly realized what he had done. God used my surrender, my faith in Him and His provision to bring Ray to repentance.

Recently, we celebrated 17 years of marriage. We still aren't perfect. But we have learned to focus on the needs of the other, over our own. Most importantly, we have learned that the love described in 1 Corinthians 13 is not the emotional love depicted by Hollywood. The God-type of love is a *behavior*, resulting from a conscious decision. Even when emotional love is gone, by making the decision to *behave* in that type of love, the emotion can and will return. It did for us.

> *Now all glory to God, who is able, through his mighty power at work within us, to accomplish infinitely more than we might ask or think. Ephesians 3:20 NLT*

Micle has experienced a walk that has steadily grown in grace. Saved at a very young age, she recommitted her life to Jesus when she was 23. Walking with Him as a worshipper, she began to expose her innermost heart to the Lord when she was 34; experiencing depths of love and knowledge she never expected. Today, Micle's passion is worship; with a special gift for prophetic worship. She is a regional operations manager for a multi-national pharmaceutical company, traveling about 80% of the time. When she isn't flying from city to city, this Texas gal currently lives in Indiana with her husband Ray and their dog, Chico.

— CHAPTER 7 —

Sustained with Joy

BY ASHLEY

If your instructions hadn't sustained me with joy, I would have died in my misery. Psalm 119:92 NLT

Five years ago, we were living in Indianapolis, Ind., with our 2-year-old son, in our new home, celebrating Ryan's new job with the fire department. I was also pregnant with our second child.

Life was good!

When I was 17 weeks pregnant, I went to the first ultrasound. That's where I found out the sex of the baby. It was a girl. I went to the bathroom and sobbed, because I really wanted a boy.

I returned to the exam room to meet with the doctor, not knowing that she would tell me something that would really make me cry. This would be much more serious. The doctor proceeded to tell me that the baby had some "water pockets on her brain." It could possibly be nothing, but she wanted me to go see a specialist right away. So I did.

They did the ultrasound and the tech noticed the baby's hands. I can remember just laying there, frozen, as she told me it was Trisomy 18, a chromosome disorder. I honestly cannot remember what was going through my head, or the proper sequence of events that happened after that. They started to talk of amniocentesis and blood work.

I called Ryan sobbing, and he rushed over to the clinic in his soaking wet gear completely disheveled. My head was spinning. We sat through meetings with at-risk doctors and counselors. When we finally got the results from all the testing and blood work, we had already settled our hearts on the reality of having to plan a funeral for our child.

A couple weeks later, I got a call from my doctor after she received all the testing. By this time I was 20 weeks.

"You need to make a decision on what to do with the baby because you only have two more weeks for an abortion to be performed," she said. "I would highly suggest you do this since you are so young and probably want to get on with your family planning. The baby will probably not make it past 22 weeks anyways ... blah, blah, blah."

I began to contemplate this horrible plan. The more I thought about going through a whole pregnancy and not having a baby to show for it was completely devastating. This totally ruined "our" plans for a family. But God rescued me immediately from these destructive thoughts.

I got up and started calling family, filling them in on the details. I would stay up late doing research and spending hours sobbing.

Surprisingly, I was not blaming God or questioning. I remember thinking many times, "Why am I not upset with God or mad at him?" To me it just seemed like I should be so angry and yet "peace surpassed all understanding."

I just began relying on all the promises that God had instilled in me in my youth. God had promised he had plans to prosper me, not to harm me. If I trust in Him, and not in my own understanding, He will direct my path. There is good in all things. God just kept running all these things through my head and heart.

I had been praying for years that God would touch my family in a miraculous way. What if this baby, who we named Madison, was created for them? I could do this if people came to know Jesus through her precious life. I could make sense of it if that were to happen. That revelation gave me much peace and happiness.

We were going to have this baby. I began to enjoy Madison and treat her as if she could be a miracle baby. I bought clothes for her. I prepared for her to come home. Every day at 4 p.m., I would lie down to tickle my belly and Madison would respond by kicking.

And it seemed the doctors kept giving me hope that she would make it. We met with NICU staff at the hospital in preparation for her arrival, just in case. We had chosen to have a respirator there for delivery until family arrived to see her. We had also set up funeral arrangements. We were prepared to say goodbye or bring her home.

I remember it was the St. Patrick's Day parade and I was 39 weeks. After the parade I went to the doctor. Madison had no heartbeat.

As much as I felt I had prepared myself, it still felt like the world had crashed around me. We scheduled induction for the next day.

On the way home, I made phone calls to family. I got home and prepared myself for the hospital. I finished making final funeral preparations.

I opened the Bible for a verse for this situation. I continually had this feeling that I needed to give her some kind of life, meaning, purpose. God had to create her for something besides death. Ryan and I came across Galatians 1:15.

> *"But even before I was born, God chose me and called me by his marvelous grace." NLT*

On March 18, I held my baby girl. She was 6 lbs. — not 2 lbs. She looked like a normal sleeping baby. She did not have the physical characteristics of T18 babies.

I thanked God that I did not have to put her on a respirator, because I could not have pulled that plug. God knew that about me. There are so many things that God spared me from. He knew I had to prepare to set her free, because I am not strong enough to lose a child suddenly.

No one in my family changed their life for Christ, but I am OK with that. I still have hope for them.

Perhaps Madison was created only to prepare me for my future beautiful little girl, Isabel, born in 2007. After Madison, Ryan got accepted on at Mishawaka Fire Department near family in South Bend, Ind. We sold our house and bought another one within two months. We have a great church. My son is in a great school. And we had our fourth child, Violet, in May of 2011.

God is good! Life is good!

Ashley is a busy, stay-at-home mom for her firefighter husband, Ryan, and their three children, Connor, Isabel and Violet. She is deeply and passionately involved in Elsie Rogers Elementary School's PTO and Southgate Church. Ashley has a degree in social work, and has worked in the mental health field for nine years. She loves to read, write and organize.

— CHAPTER 8 —

Darkness Exposed; Exchanged for Truth, Light and Life

BY SOFIA

Even after many years of layer after layer being peeled away, I still had deep wounds left behind due to the sexual abuse I endured as an adolescent.

Finally, I had engaged in the journey of healing that God prepared me for all along. Finally, I stopped shrugging it off by saying, and actually believing, that I was fine — I had already "dealt with it."

At the time I was teaching overseas, living completely out of my comfort zone, and blessed with a kindred spirit friendship. I was ripe for a healing that God would soon begin in me. Once the challenge to walk in emotional health was offered to me, I grasped it and engaged full force. There, in a safe American, Christian community (in the truest sense of community), set in a South American country, I began to expose darkness. I also began to allow others "in" to me, and began to allow those who were worthy of that level of trust to speak into and over me.

I would love to say it was dreamy, lovely and a sweet experience, but although there were moments of each of those things, the process was long, painful, grueling and lonely.

During my healing, I was challenged in a multifaceted way. Do I, or do I not, confront and expose the perpetrator (my brother-in-law)? How do I create boundaries in familial relationships? How do I trust God completely when He allowed all of this to transpire? Will I ever be able to climb out of this pit of depression that all of this seeking of healing has pushed me into?

Although this testimony could be spent primarily on how God pursued me and gave me wisdom in all those areas, there is yet another layer to be peeled away ... in the right timing, for the right reasons, in the right place and with the right people.

***

Fast-forward 10 years, back in the States and now married to a tender, compassionate and godly man, I ask a friend to pray with me over an issue. It's a sexual issue, one indirectly related to my abuse, but not obviously so. We begin praying in one direction, and God shows up, leads my friend down a different path, and what I had laid to rest as impossible was now being asked of me.

"Huh, ahem, God, you want me to what? Go to my brother-in-law, with my husband's covering, 300 miles away, and talk to him about what he did?"

Only God could have aligned this. Firstly, for me to have the kind of trust in this friend to know that she was hearing from God was supernatural. Trust does not come easy to me.

Secondly, to resonate with this, to hear and know my Father's voice, was unmistakable.

Thirdly, to have the humility and courage to approach Todd (not my brother-in-law's real name), after 30 years of allowing darkness to have its way, was just not something I was capable of mustering up on my own.

And, lastly, possibly one of the most important components, to call my husband on the phone and ask him to be my covering in this, to which he immediately said, "Yes."

Never would I have imagined that this is where God would lead when I asked my friend to come and pray with me. And, never could I have prepared for the amazing story that lie ahead — one that would expose darkness and bring freedom to many people.

It was set, after seeking God for a week, and while my sister, Emily, was in Texas helping her daughter with her newborn baby, Bryan (my husband, renamed) and I drove 300 miles to talk to Todd. Although we had prepared in advance, the closer we got to Todd and Emily's house, the more I began to unravel, freak out and walk closely with fear and doubt.

The anxiety as we drove up their driveway, knowing that in seconds Bryan would be approaching the door, cannot be described. In retrospect, clearly the enemy did not want this to take place.

My husband, my hero, left me trembling in the car, praying and texting my other sister (who had her small group praying at that moment for this encounter), while he bravely rang the doorbell.

As Todd opened the door, Bryan greeted him with, "You sexually abused Sofia when she was an adolescent."

Nodding in agreement, and holding his hand over the phone receiver with his wife, my sister, on the other end, Todd said, "Yes, I have been waiting for you to come!"

Meanwhile, sitting in an idling car, I almost jumped out of my skin as a half-foot of ice, which had come loose on the car roof, slid down and crashed to the ground. My mind was racing in a million directions, all laced with irrational fear, as my husband remained in Todd's house. Having no idea of the humble exchange that was taking place, I was outside, in a locked car, entertaining thoughts of Todd being violent to my husband, and me driving off to alert police. More irrational thoughts, more ramping up of emotions, then Bryan appears in the doorway motioning me inside.

Gulp! "No way!" I mouthed the words, multiple times.

But, to no avail, Bryan showed up at my window, where I hesitantly slid the window down. He told me it was okay, and it would be safe. Todd had taken responsibility for his actions; Todd wanted to apologize to me. Never, ever, ever had I envisioned or prepared for this. I felt paralyzed, stuck to the seat; no way could I, nor would I move.

Next thing you know, I was being gently led into the house by my dear, courageous husband. Tentatively, with Bryan by my side, I met Todd as I walked through the door. Todd stood there broken and teary eyed. But what struck me immediately was that his countenance had changed. He had gone through something — something that brought humility and sorrow and repentance. I cautiously listened as he spoke, through tears, just how wrong he had been, how sorry he was, and verbally wondered if I could possibly forgive him.

How I even began to process this long-awaited, but never-hoped-for apology is a blurred memory. Each time I even allowed myself to dream about this confrontation, my fears turned it into a catastrophe. The common thread in each fantasy was that Todd would deny ever hurting me. That he would mock me and say that I was mistaken, insecure and had a wild imagination. This allowed Satan to continue to traffic in darkness. Yes, there was immense healing, which required the painful process of layers being peeled away, one layer at a time. However, there was still this secret. My brother-in-law was still protected, my sister was still protected, and I was still allowing this lie to affect me. It also affected family dynamics, including my relationship with my sister.

That night, I calmly shared with Todd exactly what he had done, how it made me feel, and how it has negatively affected my life. I was brief, not becoming too vulnerable to him, but I blessed him with forgiveness, a process I had begun long before that night. His obvious repentance made this moment feel safer, more secure. By nature, I am very skeptical and for obvious reasons, have trust issues; however, I discerned that this was real. He truly had been waiting for this, for this very moment, asking for and receiving my forgiveness. Our spirits were changed. There was light. There was hope. There was truth!

In the spirit realm, I envisioned the angels singing, all the saints rejoicing and Jesus being so pleased with His children. Pleased by the grace, compassion, forgiveness, courage, kindness and love. Pleased that darkness was exposed and light was able to shine through, despite the garbage that was intended to destroy.

Fifteen minutes after I hesitantly let Bryan lead me in that house, the three of us stood, hand in hand, praying. Praying a sealing of what God had begun, praying for wisdom, praying for peace, and expressing our thankfulness to our healer.

We drove away changed people. Our hearts, although full of emotion, were full. Our faith was increased to a new level. My belief of God's love for me was catapulted. Truly, I had experienced the goodness of God in a way I could not have even imagined.

Oh, and what happened next ... the unthinkable. Todd called his wife (my sister), where she was out of state at their daughter's house. He told her he was taking a flight out the next day (paying more than $800 for a spur-of-the-moment flight); he had something important to share with her. Before boarding that plane, he met with his pastor and resigned from a youth ministry position he had held for several years. Revealing his heart, he shared with him what had happened in the past, and why he was stepping down. The pastor listened intently, ultimately denying his resignation. His behavior was in the past, and he was a changed man, thanks to the work of the cross. Beautiful.

If you have not yet realized God's orchestration in all of this, read on.

Remember my sister's small group that had been praying while I sat in that car? They, too, lived in the city where Emily was visiting her daughter. She and her husband picked Todd up from the airport, prayed with him, encouraged him and drove him to see his wife.

His wife, after being told, went through a multitude of emotions. After returning home, they received godly counseling, individually as well as maritally. What Satan meant to destroy, God used for good!

During a conversation I had with Emily a few weeks later, she shared that although his admission was excruciatingly painful, their marriage was healing and there was a new level of depth. Talking through this with openness and honesty was bringing them into a deeper place and love in their marriage. Incredible!

My friend, who prayed with me and heard from God that day, left me with a powerful thought that I will never forget.

"Satan is only allowed to traffic in darkness!" His lies need to be exposed and exchanged for truth, light and life!

I'm praying this powerful story will bring great hope to all who read it. Remember, where you have no hope, you are believing a lie. There is always hope. God is very, very good and creative outside of anything you could ever dream or imagine!

Sofia lives in northern Indiana with her husband. They are both artists and teachers. Together they enjoy weekend getaways and exploring the world together.

— CHAPTER 9 —

Healed Through Prayer

BY TAMERA

In late December of 2010, I began to experience numbness and tingling in my left pinky and ring fingers and up through the wrist as well. Assuming I had slept in the wrong position, I decided to sleep on my back instead.

Over the next five weeks my symptoms grew worse. I lost strength in my left hand and was unable to perform simple tasks at work like hanging pants on the hangers which you have to pinch to open and close, pulling carts around and folding clothes. It felt as though my hand had been smashed in a door.

My concern grew as the weakness in my hand became greater, and I made an appointment with my family physician. I told him of my symptoms. He did a few simple tests and suspected a pinched ulnar nerve, most likely in the elbow region.

I was then referred to an osteopathic surgeon who did more in-depth tests for strength in my hand. He was pretty certain that I would need to surgically have the ulnar nerve relocated, but needed to order an electromyogram test (EMG) to pinpoint the exact location of the problem.

While looking up the surgical procedure online, I became frightened. It spoke of not being able to work for at least eight weeks and then needing physical therapy to regain strength in my hand, and that depending on the type of surgery that would be performed, total healing would take six months to a year.

I was so upset and annoyed that so quickly I had lost strength in my hand and was unable to perform my job. I also dreaded the thought of not being able to use my left hand for eight plus weeks. As a side, I am working on a fiction novel. I did not want to believe this was happening to me.

As I waited for the EMG appointment, I began requesting prayers for healing from friends and family. I also had special prayer at church one day, where I went to the front and had people come and lay hands on and pray for me. Over the next week I experienced less and less tingling and pain in my left hand and arm.

I went to Michiana Spine, Sports and Occupational Rehab in mid-February to have the EMG test, but the doctor did not find any problem with the ulnar nerve at my elbow, or in my wrist. He wanted to send me for an MRI to check the C8 disk in the neck to see if that was the source of the problem. Due to limited medical insurance, I knew there was no way I could afford to have that done. As I debated whether or not to have that test done, the symptoms continued to subside, even as people continued to pray for me. The numbness, pain and tingling went away, yet I still wondered if I would regain my strength.

As I write this, one year has passed and I have no symptoms. I have regained all the strength in my hand and am able to perform my job. Surgery was not needed because the God I serve can restore, recreate, heal and make all things new again. I want to thank all family, friends and fellow church members who prayed for my healing.

With God, all things are possible.

Tamera lives in the Michiana area with her husband, John, and their two children. She spent her childhood moving around the United States, and attended 16 schools, kindergarten through 10th grade. After having been out of school for 10 years, Tamera earned her GED and began classes at IUSB where she earned degrees in communications and English. She presently works at a popular Michiana department store, and is waiting on the Lord to move her into her chosen career.

— CHAPTER 10 —

His Perfection Covers Me

BY ERIN

"You are a terrible housekeeper," he said.

The words echoed in my brain. "Yes, I am. You're right," I said shamefully.

"You are lazy, messy and a procrastinator. You're a bad wife and mom. Is this the example you want to give to your daughter?"

"No," I said, feeling terribly guilty.

When would I get it right? When would I pull myself out of my funk and be one of those people who could keep up with all the little things on a daily basis?

I constantly struggled to find new methods to organize myself — new ways of creating daily routines, new ways to motivate myself to stay on top of it all. I would find a new system and be optimistic that finally, this would be the thing that would work for me. And inevitably, it wasn't. I always found myself at the bottom of the pit again, terrified that someone would come to my house and see the mess.

It wasn't that my house was really that terrible — it wasn't like the hoarders show on cable TV — but I never felt that I measured up to the standard. And the truth was that I did procrastinate. I made choices such as watching TV when I should have been cleaning up the kitchen or folding the laundry.

And then one day, somehow, God quietly began to break through.

I grew up in church and had an active relationship with God from the time I was 11 years old. I knew everything a Christian should know, and yet, ironically, I had missed the relevance of the gospel for me. Even though I didn't struggle with the "big sins," I was shocked to discover that I was still wallowing in the prison of self-condemnation.

I never realized the depth of the conversations taking place in my head, where "he" told me that I was messy, lazy, a procrastinator, and a bad wife and mom. "He" was a combination of Satan's accusations and my own poor self-esteem. I realized that it didn't take much for Satan to set me on a course of self-destruction because I readily agreed with his lies.

When God began to break through, I slowly dared to believe that He could love me anyway; that I could live in a messy state for the rest of my life and He would love me no matter what. I awakened to the depth of His grace in my life. I gradually came to realize who I am in Christ — the reality that Jesus' blood covers me every day, and He covers my mistakes and my sin — even the sin of laziness.

I also realized that I had to let go of perfectionism; I had let go of what I thought others expected of me; and, most of all, I had to let go of accepting myself as a victim.

You see, there was part of this equation that had been working for me. When I accepted the title of "procrastinator" or "bad housekeeper," I gave myself permission to make those kinds of choices. I'll never forget the moment the Holy Spirit revealed this to me — I was sitting in church, listening to a sermon, and I almost yelled for joy right in the middle of what the pastor was saying. You know it is the Holy Spirit convicting you, and not condemnation from yourself or the enemy, when you get excited over the revelation of sin in your life!

Now, God is teaching me that I am empowered. I am His. I have authority. I am covered by grace. In the last two years He has given me numerous revelations, some big and some little, that have gradually led me to freedom.

On a recent Sunday night, I came home to a messy house. "You are a terrible housekeeper," something whispered in my head. "If you hadn't been lazy earlier today, you wouldn't have this mess to deal with."

"No," I replied. "I'm not a terrible housekeeper, and I'm not lazy. I made a choice earlier today to rest, and I'm okay with that choice. Just because my house is messy at this moment does not mean that I am a procrastinator and a lazy person."

At that point I turned to God and admitted that I felt overwhelmed at the current state of my house. But instead of linking up with a negative feeling, I asked God, "How can I turn this around and empower myself?"

I immediately realized that I could set my timer for 20 minutes (a technique I frequently use when cleaning up) and focus on picking up the house, and after that time I would probably feel much better about my circumstances.

But you know what? I chose not to. I was exhausted, physically and mentally. And I chose to sit and relax instead.

I went to bed that night without a hint of condemnation or feelings of depression over the state of my house. The next day I set my timer for 20 minutes and I cleaned up, and again there were no condemning thoughts of, "if you had only done this yesterday, you wouldn't have to do it now — this is more evidence that you are a procrastinator." Instead, I felt empowered.

I realize now how destructive the cycle of self-condemnation can be. Guilt and shame are never effective motivators for lasting change. While they did push me to take action, the results were not constructive. If my actions were positive (such as cleaning up when things were messy), then the result was the feeling that it was a nice try, but it wasn't really good enough. If my actions were negative (such as sitting and not doing anything) I was sucked further into a cycle of depression and inactivity.

Now, I shrug off guilt and shame and I ask God to tell me the truth about the situation and about myself. Sometimes I don't like the answer; sometimes He tells me that I am being lazy and I have to confront the reality of my own choices. I have to deal with habits that have been formed, and do the work of changing those habits.

I am still not perfect at keeping house. But that's OK, because His perfection covers me.

But He said to me,

> "My grace is sufficient for you, for my power is made perfect in weakness." Therefore I will boast all the more gladly about my weaknesses, so that Christ's power may rest on me. That is why, for Christ's sake, I delight in weaknesses, in insults, in hardships, in persecutions, in difficulties. For when I am weak, then I am strong. 2 Corinthians 12:9-10 NIV

Erin is a wife, a mom, a marketer, a recovering slob, and would like to believe she is an avid reader and gourmet cook. After growing up in a Christian home and living the standard Christian life, she was surprised to discover just how much she really does need the gospel. She works at Bethel College as the assistant director of marketing, and on evenings and weekends she sells Starfish Jewelry and is a social media consultant.

— CHAPTER 11 —

The Heart of a Mother; a Restored Family

BY NICKOLETTE

I believe God uses everything for His glory, and I believe not having a mom around gave me a heart's desire to be a mom from a very young age. As I grew that desire grew, then God expanded it ...

I started out life as the youngest of two. My older brother and I were raised by my father, who tried very hard to be both mother and father to us — he did a pretty good job. He even sewed my dresses, but I just knew there was something missing.

When I was 6, my dad remarried. That's when I realized that having a mom was not necessarily the fairytale dream I once believed.

Through the years I began to understand that blood doesn't make you a mom, it's the daily care and commitment that earns you that name, but I still had that hole in my heart for my biological mother.

Growing up I always had a sense of the Lord's presence and protection in my life, but wasn't sure what it was till I got older. Now I know that God used my childhood to mold me into what He wanted me to be.

As I grew, my desire was always the same — I wanted to be a mom. In elementary school, I learned that being a mom was not a "career," so I told teachers I wanted to be a nurse so I could take care of all the babies.

In high school, I thought, "Hmmm, I could be a missionary like my grandma and grandpa, and go over seas to take care of all the poor orphans of the world."

So in speech class my sophomore year, we were to write a speech about what we wanted to do with our lives when we grew up, and I wrote my speech about being a missionary overseas. That's when God revealed what He wanted to do with my life. I was to be a mother to the motherless right here in the U.S., and I knew then I would become a foster parent and show God's love to His children.

I made many mistakes during my late teens and early 20s; I was just so anxious to start my life, the one God showed me. I was going to have two kids, one boy, one girl, and foster and adopt the rest, but first I had to get married, right? Lord I need a man, one that would fit the criteria!

Well, I set out to find my man. I moved faster than God, or was just too busy to hear Him. I got married and I gave birth to our son. I am finally a mother! It was the one of happiest days of my life. In fact, I couldn't sleep for five days straight. Then two-and-a-half years later, I had our daughter. God you are so amazing!

Now my mission was to start — my husband and I got our foster care license and received our first foster child when my daughter was 6 months old. For six years we fostered many kids and took guardianship of three. I enjoyed showing God's love to them all.

Then my world started to crumble. My marriage fell apart. Now what Lord? I am a single mother. I wasn't receiving any foster care funding any longer, due to having full guardianship, and I didn't have a job, as I was always a stay-at-home mom.

I felt I had failed. My life would never be what I dreamt or even what God had intended. Now I am struggling alone to raise all these kids. Where are you Lord? He was there nudging me along, I see now. Little did I know He was using my mess to bring me to a point where I had to release the grip I had on my life and give it back Him. I had nowhere else to turn but to Him. Oh Lord, forgive me for wanting to do life my way. He gave me the desire, the vision and the ability, but I took over. God has a plan for our lives, but it only works if we yield to His Spirit and not rely on our own strength and desires.

Soon God brought along a helpmate, my husband, Dan, who also went through his own trials of a broken marriage. Between the two of us we had quite the quiver of kids; we had my two, his three and the ones I had guardianship of. Only through God's strength were we able to merge such a diverse group together.

We continued to show God's love to several more children we took in along the way, and God blessed us with three more biological babies together. If you lost count, which we often do, there are 14 kids that call us mom and dad. Not only is it our heart for the kids to see God through us, but also the families of the kids we took in. It has been quite a long and twisty road, but God has been faithful and full of blessings.

Through this chapter of our lives we began to see ourselves as a family of restoration. This became our mission. We believe God wants to use us to help others restore what man, time and circumstances have torn apart. God has wonderful plans for our lives even when we get in the way and mess it up. All we have to do is ask for His forgiveness, yield to His Spirit and give it all over to Him. Then He can take our mess and turn it into something usable.

Nickolette is a mother to the motherless. She grew up without her mother, but God took her pain and replaced it with a heart of compassion. She is married to Dan and together they have 14 children who call them mom and dad; currently there are eight who call them grammy and grandpa. Nickolette stays home with the kids and is homeschooling the youngest three. She doesn't have much time for hobbies, but she does raise West Highland White Terriers, in which she truly enjoys.

— CHAPTER 12 —

Through Life's Struggles, God Breaks Through

BY PEGGY

My story starts with a childhood that no child should have to live through. Unfortunately, there were not many happy memories.

I was raised in a Presbyterian church until about the age of 12. My mom took me, my sister and brother every Sunday with her. My dad never went to church. Although we attended church every week, we never talked about God. I didn't have a clue about God. I couldn't say I believed in God. This "limbo" type of living went on for many years; I never really felt like I belonged anywhere or with anyone. I just existed.

My dad was a violent alcoholic and that affected me and my life tremendously. I started feeling like I wasn't loved or even wanted in my family. I suffered verbal, physical and sexual abuse from many people during this time of my life. After each instance I felt the same: unworthy of anyone's love, shame, guilt, unloved and misplaced. Those feelings started determining my path.

As the years went by, I got married and divorced twice, had a child and got into another relationship. I always felt like I was missing something. I was always searching for something or someone to make me feel better.

My daughter started using drugs and alcohol and went to a girls' school in Arizona. I was still seeking the attention and love that I never felt I got from my parents, and I was familiar with looking for that attention in all of the wrong places with the wrong people.

I soon got tangled up with an internet romance and found myself pregnant at the age of 40. I knew I was not capable of raising another child at that time in my life. I decided I was going to have an abortion because I didn't feel there was any other option. Little did I know that this decision would haunt me and keep me "locked up" for a very long time. Those memories have never gone away. In fact, I can remember every detail as if it happened yesterday. I can honestly say it was the worst day of my entire life; worse than all of the abuse and feelings that I had ever felt previously or afterward.

At 18, my daughter returned home and I decided I needed help in parenting and I recognized that I was still seeking out that "something and/or someone" to fill the void in my heart. I started seeing a therapist. She invited me to church.

The first day I decided to attend, the enemy really worked against me. I thought I knew where the church was, but to my discovery, I didn't. I ended up about 10 miles away. By this time I was going to be late, but I called the church and was told that it didn't matter if I was late as people came and went at all times during the service. He gave me directions from where I was, and off in the other direction I headed. I then got stopped by not one, but two trains. After the second train and almost 30 minutes late to service, I was welcomed with loving arms as I walked into church.

I felt immediate peace — like I was where I was meant to be. I felt the love that I had been seeking for many years. My therapist had told me that if I sat in the back pew no one would "bombard" me with questions, wanting to talk, etc. They would just "leave me alone." That pew was my safe haven.

As time went on, a few people welcomed me, shook my hand, gave me many hugs and confirmed to me that I was where I needed to be. One day a lady came up to me, sat down with me and prayed over me. WOW! It was truly amazing, the love I felt. I later discovered that she was carrying God's love to me. It was the love that I had sought after for so many years right there — embracing me. It felt like I was in a field of wild flowers experiencing unconditional love and peace.

Through the years I have had many trials and tribulations. I've sought after God to direct me in the decisions and events. For the first time in some 20 years, I felt peace with my daughter's life. I didn't like that she was doing drugs, drinking alcohol and continuing in a physically abusive relationship; but with the love of God, I was able to turn my daughter over to Him. I could no longer carry the burden of her life and choices.

I got remarried in March of 2007 and soon our family grew. In October of that same year, we accepted guardianship of my daughter's two children. Although this was a challenge, it was also a blessing from God.

After about three years, my daughter finally got tired of running from everything, getting high, being abused and running from the police for outstanding warrants. She was arrested and she served her time.

She is now a recovering addict and I couldn't be happier for her. I am very proud of her accomplishments as well as my own. Today, I no longer have to handle everything life sends me alone. I have the Lord Jesus Christ to turn to in time of need.

I would also like to say that recently as I was driving home from a Narcotics Anonymous meeting, I heard God tell me that my aborted child was a girl and her name was Nicole Elizabeth. He also told me that she forgives me for aborting her and that she loves me. We will see each other in heaven. This, I believe, completed the healing process of having the abortion. God forgave me, I forgave myself and Nicole Elizabeth forgave me — by the grace of God.

Peggy is a wife, mother and grandmother who lives in Culver, Ind. She has been living her dream as a secretary for many years and hopes to continue doing so. She is married to a very hard-working man who is the light of her eye, on most days! Peggy has a 10-year-old dog named Buttercup who is her baby. Just last year, she was coerced by her granddaughters to adopt a stray kitten whom they named Rosemont (Rosie, although it is a male). She loves the places of healing that God has been taking her to and looks forward to many more journeys with Him.

— CHAPTER 13 —

Honor Restores Father-Daughter Relationship

BY TRECIA

I stood there with my best friend from kindergarten staring at the Jumbo-Tron. A picture of Bible teacher Joyce Meyer baptizing her 80-year-old father was on the screen. It was like I was deaf to every other sound except for the voice of the Lord and his quiet whisper to my heart, "It's time."

I had been a Christian my whole life and I loved God. But He was asking something of me that was terrifying. We had come to St. Louis for the annual Women's Convention just to hang out and spend time at the feet of Joyce, to get renewed and re-energized before returning to our lives as women, wives and moms. But what God wanted to do in me would completely change my life as I knew it.

My dad hadn't wanted to get married so young. The oldest of 10 children, raised by a philandering, angry and abusive father, my dad longed to be free. But his girlfriend ended up pregnant. So after unsuccessfully trying to convince her to have an abortion and convince everyone else that the child wasn't his, my parents married when Dad was only 19.

Feeling trapped and angry, the abuse of my mom and her new baby, my brother, began immediately. Another brother was born into the misery two years later, and by the time news of my conception came along three years after that, he had a pretty serious mistress with whom he had hoped to escape his domestic prison.

He tried to talk my mother into aborting me. I've been told that he never wanted to hold me and pretty much didn't until I was about 18 months old. Considering the beatings that my siblings endured from him, I've always considered that a blessing. But, it does something to a child to not be wanted by their own father.

They tell me that I used to follow him around. I think I developed my out-going nature from trying to get his attention and approval. Just a theory! But it's a fact that the lack of a father in my life — one who was crazy about me or even cared that I breathed — completely shaped my dating relationships.

I was certainly taken advantage of by guys who were "only after one thing," but as I think back, I feel sorry for some of those teenage boys who could never live up to my unrealistic expectation that they would love me unconditionally, and give me the love I so desperately wanted and had never felt from my dad.

Once my mom remarried, my dad lost all interest entirely. We still would visit his mom, our grandmother, and honor her. Sometimes we would run into him at her house.

He would spend a few minutes saying, "God, it's good to see you," and a generic "I'm sorry," before he launched in a diatribe of how horrible my mom was. The same mom that worked one to two jobs at a time for nine years, never making more than $10,000 a year, yet providing us with food, clothing, shelter and a godly upbringing.

So we, the kids, would say, "Well, you can't talk about mom like that. It's been nice seeing you. SEE ya!"

Years would go by, running the same scenario again and again, till 20 years had passed.

And so, there I stood, looking up at the Jumbo-Tron picture of Joyce Meyer baptizing her father. This man, who had sexually abused her for 13 years, was born again, a new creation. And he was different, Joyce said. After all those years, at age 80, he finally admitted he had hurt her and was sorry and asked her for forgiveness.

So, I thought, if she could forgive him for all that abuse, couldn't I find a way to forgive my dad? Couldn't I find some way to obey God by "honoring my father?" I stood there, heart pounding, crying and made a commitment to God that I would reach out to my dad.

I wrote and rewrote many letters. I found that when you're hurt, it's really hard not to point the finger at people, even in a letter. Finally, after piles of crumpled paper, I narrowed the focus of my letter, saying that I didn't want anything from him. I didn't want money. I didn't need anything. I just wanted a chance to get to know him, to get to know my half-sisters, and have some kind of relationship with him. I told him that I forgave him and that he was free of any debt he owed me.

And as per Joyce Meyer, I sent him gifts! She says that forgiveness is an action, not just words. So, I sent him a Joyce Meyer daily calendar with excerpts from her messages, along with some coffee and coffee mugs. I prayed over the box, and sent it along with my note that had my mobile number and address in case he wanted to contact me.

He called me a few days after Christmas. What an unbelievable present! The call was off to a great start, but five minutes in, just like in all the times before, he started to go after my mom.

But I wasn't a kid anymore, and I told him that I knew about the women, the drinking and the abuse. And it wasn't just mom telling me about it, but I'd heard it from his friends. I mentioned a few names, and I guess he realized I knew what I was talking about.

He said, "Well, yeah, I guess there were women."

Ta-Da! I can't tell you how much his honesty about just that one thing gave me the will to keep the conversation going. I pressed him about abusing my two brothers and mother.

Silence.

There, I'd done it. Complete silence on the other end. Then he started to get really defensive, denied ever being abusive and it looked like he was going to bail. In my heart, I cried out to God for wisdom.

The Lord put the words in my mouth and I heard myself saying, "You know what? We are never going to agree on the past. Why don't we just have a rule that we don't talk about it? We have a chance to know each other and be a part of each other's lives NOW. What do you say?"

And he went for it! Praise the Lord! We kept talking and I found out a lot about him, especially what I hadn't known about his battle with cancer and several heart attacks. I got up-to-speed on his daughters, my young adult sisters, who I hadn't been around since the time they were toddlers!

We ended the phone call both committing to keep in touch. The hardest part for me was just beginning, though.

Now I had to tell my family what I had done. I started by showing my mom and then my brothers a copy of the letter I had sent to dad. Then I explained what had happened since. None of them could really understand why I would want to have anything to do with the guy we had always referred to as "the monster." I had no reason except for God's Word.

> *Honor your father and mother. Exodus 20:12 NIV*

> *Whoever claims to love God yet hates a brother or sister [or father!] is a liar! For whoever does not love their brother and sister, whom they have seen, cannot love God, whom they have not seen. 1 John 4:20 NIV*

> *But if you do not forgive others their trespasses [their reckless and willful sins, leaving them, letting them go and giving up resentment], neither will your Father forgive you your trespasses. Matthew 6:15 AMP*

I could only do what I knew God had told me to do. Only I would stand before God and explain my treatment of my earthly father. Everyone would have to make their own choices and find their own path to forgiveness.

In the 10 years that have passed since reconciling with my dad, I have found that forgiveness has opened new realms of relationship with God. I have grown exponentially in my understanding of God's love. I have felt God so tangibly as I have let go of past hurts. Beyond a friendship with my dad, it's been such a bonus to have relationships with my half-sisters and now, their children. And the most ironic outcome is that my father, who didn't even want me, is faithful to call me every week.

I think of all that the devil meant for our harm and am so amazed at how God has worked all things for good. We talk about fishing, hunting and NASCAR. Let's just say that it's a good thing I like sports!

But we also talk about our lives. And I pray for him right there over the phone, even though he is still pre-Christian. I long to have a photo of my dad being baptized, made new through the salvation that Jesus offers. Maybe not on a Jumbo-Tron, but framed over my mantle or tucked safely in a family scrapbook would be wonderful. I pray for it and hope for it. And I continue to be kind to my dad, just as he is. Maybe the kindness he feels from me will lead him to Christ. (Romans 2:4)

This reconciliation has healed me and enabled me to love my husband and my children more fully. In exposing the painful memories and hurts, God was able to come in and bring light to parts of my character that were being ruled by the lie that I was unlovable. I was so scared to reach out to my dad. So afraid of being rejected or let down again.

But, in God's timing and with his strengthening grace, he brought his Word to pass that He will,

> *Turn the hearts of the fathers to their children, and the hearts of children to their fathers. Malachi 4:6 ESV*

If anyone reading this is on the fence about whether or not to forgive someone, to lift the burden of guilt and shame off of someone, I can tell you, it's so worth it. Though I have boundaries in place with my dad, I am living in the promised land of freedom in Christ. And I am blessed beyond all I could've dared to ever hope or imagine!

Trecia lives in Edwardsburg, Mich., with her husband and two children.

— CHAPTER 14 —

Beauty in Brokenness

BY DEANNA

It is very difficult to trust someone who hasn't suffered. What do I mean by that?

The Lord is looking for people who will carry His heart. Unfortunately most of us believers live on the surface. We may be able to speak about "meaty" issues or go deep at times, but we are unable to dwell in the depths. When we go through suffering it carves a cup of sorrow deep within us; the deeper that cup goes, the greater the capacity for Jesus to fill it with His heart. Now many may disagree with me here, but the truth is that our ability to care for others depends upon how deep we have suffered ourselves. When we go through loss or pain that shatters our heart, something DEEP happens. It doesn't happen overnight, and it is a process we must willingly submit ourselves to.

Training Through a Trial

My story arises out of an 18-year struggle (trial) with physical affliction. Having been healthy my whole life, it was difficult when things began to change. It would be too long to give details other than saying that every year brought a gradual decline from the previous year. While there were many surgeries and much, much prayer, improvement was small and temporary.

About four years into the trial, the Lord spoke to me at length. While I wrestled with anger and depression over my circumstances, He addressed the sin of unbelief. If I truly trusted Him with my life, then why was I angry? To me, freedom equaled (deliverance from physical bondage) (being healed). Jesus directed me to the realm of the Spirit saying anything He allowed in my life was to train me in the Spirit, which I had asked Him to do. He asked me to trust Him and allow Him to take my trust deeper and deeper. In this time of communion with Him, I was assured I would be healed one day.

If we are to be overcomers, then we need something to overcome. In my journey I have felt incredibly broken about not being healed physically, still knowing this promise is true and it is coming. But I now understand overcoming is of our spiritual nature, sometimes exemplified with external change. But Romans 8 has become my lifeline and my directive through the years. At His most broken, bruised and bloodied point, Jesus fulfilled His Father's will and destiny here on earth. My prayer is to fulfill His will and purpose for my life as well.

A Visitation

It was during a time of great breaking in my heart that Jesus visited me. He held an ordinary grey vase in His hand. Inside this vase I could see a flickering light, but because of the thick grey structure it was barely visible from the outside. I could see that Jesus loved this vase, so it startled me when He held it up with both hands and then dropped it. Falling to the ground, it shattered into many pieces.

As it did, I felt, "Oh my, that is how my heart feels now."

Then I heard,

> The Lord is near to the broken-hearted and saves those who are crushed in spirit. Psalm 34:18 NIV

As I heard this, Jesus looked down at the broken vessel so tenderly and with such deep compassion. Truly, I felt His sorrow in the breaking. When pain hits you hard, you have this feeling of being all alone. Instantly, I knew how close, how very close our Lord is to us in deep pain.

Next, Jesus knelt down to the vessel. Lying in broken pieces all around, it was unrecognizable except for the light that had been inside. Now the light was sitting on the ground with nothing to support it, yet nothing to close it in. Then Jesus began to work with something like a huge hand that came from above. I knew this to be the Father's hand. It was like a swirl of light and color, and though I saw this process in a matter of minutes, I knew it to be much longer in our time.

"What were they doing?" I thought.

Then I saw a vessel being formed around the light, a beautiful stained glass vase. The colors were magnificent and Father and Son were taking their time, giving very special care to this vessel as if it were the only one in the world.

As the vessel took shape, I saw words beginning to form on each segment of stained glass: love, peace, faithfulness, kindness, gentleness, goodness, self-control, long-suffering and joy.

Then came three segments that they really seemed to take their time on: purity, and I heard, "Blessed are the pure in heart for they shall see God;" Meekness, and I heard "Blessed are the meek, for they shall inherit the earth;" and Truth, "You shall know the truth and the truth shall set you free."

As these final ones were put in place, they seemed to secure the light, and then all the fruits of the spirit formed around it. Then Jesus stepped back and watched as the Father poured a golden liquid into all the segments, securing them together and completing the work.

I felt instantly in my spirit, "That is love from the Father's heart," which I heard described once as liquid golden love.

I cannot emphasize the beauty of the finished vase or the incredible love and admiration on Jesus' face when he stepped back to assess the work. Oh how He loves us!

"I am not done in or cancelled out by any means," I thought. It is the opposite!

Answers in a Jar of Clay

The Lord began to explain to me. We are jars of clay and the light is our new birth which takes place when we invite Jesus into our heart. But we still have our jar of clay, our old man, to the degree that we have not dealt with it. Jesus commands us to take up our cross and follow Him. We are told (instructed) to lose our life for His sake and He will give us a new one.

I had sought to answer this call from the Lord to the degree I was able to, asking Him what needed to go from my old self and seeking to obey. But I found my old self so hard to get rid of!

This is when Jesus said He stepped in to help me. I am not saying Jesus causes suffering at all. Suffering is in the world due to sin and the enemy. I do know that many times the Lord will divinely intervene to stop suffering, but the opposite also happens. Suffering comes to all of His children. The only difference is the degree and type of suffering we go through. What I do know is that it is hard to break our earthen vessel on our own. But until it is broken, the light of Jesus (which came at our new birth) is dim, hidden by walls of clay. The potential for great beauty exists within us and may flicker at times, but the Father's intention is to unleash it!

When I received this visit, I was 10 years into this trial which had become increasingly more difficult every year. But it was then that I felt my heart so broken I didn't know if I could go on. The Lord then showed me that there are layers of our old self — outer, inner and innermost.

Outer dying involves losing the external things we hold onto that give us false identities. This can be described as losing the bad in order to receive the good. We lose these in order to receive a newer, truer identity in Christ. The next layer is harder, but so worth it if we are willing to embrace it. It involves dying to things that are not bad, they just aren't His best for us. We also allow the Lord to speak to areas of our heart that need to be broken. There is pain here, but great fulfillment in walking closer to Jesus.

The Ultimate Breaking

Finally, the ultimate breaking is when we fellowship in the sufferings of Jesus, laying down our life for Jesus' sake alone. Involving incomparable pain, it is done simply out of obedience and love for Jesus and a desire for Him to receive glory. We give up everything in this crushing — all our hopes, dreams, desires and all of our ways. It is the ultimate cleansing that is necessary for true union with Christ. (John 14:23, Galatians 2:20) No self, no gain, no profit. This is Christlikeness in its purest expression, and the place of perfect union for which we were originally created. I know to those who undergo this breaking there is so much glory upon this vessel!

We all have the choice before us. We can go through difficult circumstances solely in the strength of our outer man. The result is that our clay vessel now has thicker walls and light within is dim. Or we can break apart during a great trial, allow Jesus to speak to certain areas and remain on the altar as stained glass is formed. However, because we have known our clay pieces for years, it is so EASY to pick them up and pin our impatience. The result is a jar of clay with segments of stained glass – a mixture of spirit and flesh.

And finally, there are those broken vessels who are remaining in the Father's hand as He gently pieces them together with His words of life and their submission to Him. These are presently being formed into GORGEOUS vessels of honor and beauty. Filled with the Father's heart they are completely transparent, with their light within fully exposed, displaying the marvelous character of Jesus Christ Himself.

Every Vessel is Unique

Then Jesus explained to me how they will always be broken in the sense that He is the vine and we are the branches, apart from Him we can do nothing. Separate pieces of glass, formed thru surrender, submission and obedience, are personally fitted together by our Lord. These are then held together by the Father's golden love which is the strongest force in all the universe!

"Oh my," I thought. "This is what Jesus desires to do in our heart if we will let Him."

It is a process over time and every vessel is unique in its suffering as well as its potential for glory. Despite the deep pain in my heart, I was so encouraged with the beauty of the vase being completed. This is how we become one with Christ, for the fragments are formed directly from this nature — He is in us and we are in Him! (John 14:23)

It is easy to run to people, places or things in time of despair and turmoil. But over and over the Lord would whisper, "It is about your vessel. Tend to your vessel."

He is gracious and merciful to us, for He is the High Priest who sympathizes with all of our pains. But He so longs to become one with us right in the midst of our pain. If we will remain broken and in the Father's hand, we will receive the greatest reward, Jesus himself formed within us in all of His glory.

> *If anyone loves Me he will keep my Word; and My Father will love him, and We will make our home with him. John 14:23 NKJV*

> *I have been crucified with Christ; it is no longer I who live, but Christ lives in me; and the life which I now live in the flesh I live by faith in the Son of God who loved me and gave Himself for me. Galatians 2:20 NKJV*

Pulling on Christ

I know that the fruits of the spirit can be cultivated by a sincere heart at any place and any time in our Christian walk. However, I have discovered that our times of need place us in a position to pull on Christ's nature within us or gravitate more toward our (earthly nature and its resources) natural resources. When we pull on Christ, He releases Himself and His spiritual resources to us. He desires to give Himself completely to us, but only to the degree that we desire Him completely!

When I am in distress I need His peace. When my enemies persecute me I need His goodness in order to bless them. When I am struggling to believe I need His faithfulness. When I am exhausted from all directions, I need His kindness toward even those that I dearly love. When I am frustrated with people and genuine issues, I need His gentleness toward them. When I am tempted to complain, I need His self-control.

I love the joy I have had thru my life when everything is going great for me. But I can say with all my heart that disappointment and discouragement have threatened joy more than any other fruit of the spirit. And the big "Ds" have succeeded I will admit.

What I discovered, however, is that true joy comes from Jesus' heart and purpose for us. It is tempting to pick up false joy, but at the end of the day disappointments and discouragement are still there. Over the years I have pressed into James 1:3, Romans 5:3-5 and I Peter 1:5-7. Moments of joy are welcomed and embraced, but deep abiding joy that transcends all emotion is the true treasure we must dig deep for.

So I advise you to buy gold from me — gold that has been purified by fire. Then you will be rich. Revelation 3:18 NLT

When I feel beaten down and unloved, I need the love of my Beloved not only to love others but to go on in the high calling. (Philippians 3:14)

And finally, I had a little long-suffering before the breaking process. But as my trial has expanded yearly, so I have found the perseverance I had is not sufficient. I confess that I have tried so many times to persevere in my natural man, picking up the broken pieces of clay and interfering with Jesus' work. But His graciousness keeps Him close, ready to run to us when we surrender our struggle. It is then that He releases Himself to us for He is our strength, and this enables us to suffer long.

Deanna lives with her husband and two sons in Osceola, Ind. Together with her husband, they oversee Voice Ministries in Elkhart. Their heart is to prepare and equip a people for the triumphal return of Jesus Christ through loving Him and loving one another. Deanna loves to be out in nature, whether at the beach, the mountains or in the middle of the acreage where they live. She loves spending time with family and watching sunsets, but most of all seeking the Lord. Though challenging, there is no greater adventure to Deanna than the quest to know the Lord in His fullness; it is what compels her forward in her life. She is also the author of "Masterpiece in the Wilderness."

— CHAPTER 15 —

Have Faith, With God Anything Is Possible in Marriage

BY JENNIFER

I am sharing my story because I want other wives who may be going through something similar to have faith that things can change. My husband and I have known each other for a little more than six years. We were both previously married and were a bit apprehensive about giving marriage another try. Both of our former spouses had addiction problems, and we did not want to put our children through any further unhappiness. However, after dating for more than a year, we were certain that this relationship was strong and we had the same goals and values. We were in love and we decided to put aside our worries to build a life together.

Unexpectedly, due to an emergency circumstance, my husband was awarded full custody of his three children. At the time, we had begun to look for houses together and the children knew we were planning to be together. We quickly found a house that was just right for our family, purchased it and moved in.

We each had full custody of our children; he had three and I had one. Instantly, we became a family of six. This was when the stress began. Neither of us had been a full-time parent of four children before. We had different parenting styles. We began to have small disagreements.

Two years after moving into our house, we decided to make things official and get married. This was something that I was ready for, but later found out that my husband was really still terrified at the thought of being married — as if the actual marriage commitment would result in the demise of our relationship.

My husband began to change. He became agitated and moody. He was unhappy most of the time and began to find fault with everything that I or the children did. I started to question my decision to re-marry. I would talk to God every morning as I drove to work and ask Him to help me. I prayed that I had made the right decision for myself, my son and my husband's children.

Then, we began to have large disagreements. The arguments were often loud. Most of the time, our arguments were happening at night. The kids were in bed and their sleep was disturbed. They were beginning to be stressed out.

I was beside myself. It didn't seem to matter what I did, I could not avoid an argument. It seemed that my husband was negative all of the time. He was angry over finances, though we had no real financial difficulties at all. He was irate over parenting differences. He was resentful about not being sexually satisfied. He made me feel like a failure.

On mornings after these arguments, I would cry in the shower (so the kids couldn't hear me) as I got ready for work. I was losing faith that our marriage was ever the right decision. I prayed for God to help me get out of this situation. I asked God to give me a sign; tell me what to do. I didn't want to hurt anyone by leaving, and I was beginning to think that staying with my husband was no longer possible. I felt alone and hopeless. I did not feel like God was listening.

I began to have negative thoughts about our relationship. It didn't help that my husband was constantly threatening to divorce me. He would throw his wedding ring across the room. He would tell me that our marriage was the "worst mistake he ever made." He would sleep on the floor or the couch. He would call me terrible names and say things that were hurtful and mean. But, he would usually apologize soon afterward and send flowers to my workplace. I was starting to dislike flowers.

I begged my husband to go to counseling with me. I felt that our marriage was on the brink of divorce. I told him I couldn't continue to live the way that we were living. At first, my husband balked at the idea of counseling. He was certain that things would just work out. Finally, after several very trying months, he agreed to go to a marriage counselor.

The counselor was recommended to us by a family member. She

was insightful and offered a lot of good advice. My husband listened to her suggestions and tried to implement them at home. We went to counseling for a year-and-a-half with little success. Our counselor said that our relationship was like a "roller coaster" and that she could not accomplish much if my husband was unwilling to admit that he had anger issues and that he was verbally abusive. My husband was unwilling to admit that most of the fault was his.

In the meantime, I began to attend our church more regularly. My son was a member of the youth group and he went every week. I was raised in the Catholic Church and had a difficult time getting used to our nondenominational church.

Church became another regular topic of arguments. My husband resented me going to church every Sunday morning because he claimed it was damaging our sex life — apparently I should have been staying home on Sunday mornings to have sex. He also felt like I was pressuring him to attend church, even though I never tried to pressure him. We had discussed church and he had agreed that he wanted to take our kids to church, but apparently that was something he said to make me happy at the time.

I felt like I needed church. I needed to be around others who were praying even when things seemed hopeless. I felt closer to God at our church than any place else, and I prayed every Sunday for Him to help me, help my son, help my husband and help my step-children. I went to church each week, knowing that I would hear criticism from my husband, because I needed to be closer to God in some way.

Finally, after two years of marriage and a year-and-a-half of marriage counseling, my husband began to become hateful. He told me I was ugly. He said that I was not the mother of HIS kids and had no right to discuss them with him (even though we were raising all of our kids together). He screamed and yelled. He accused me of outrageous things. I could count on having an argument — usually about sex — every Sunday night around 10 p.m. or later. I was exhausted. I was suffering from migraines. My son was asking why we weren't moving out. It was horrible.

Then, the worst argument happened right before Christmas. I was shopping for presents for our children when my husband called me. At first, he was friendly. Then, he became angry. He yelled through the cell phone that I was a lesbian and a whore. He told me to move out immediately. He said that I was not welcome at HIS family's Christmas, and neither was my son.

He screamed "I hate you! I hate you!" over and over hysterically.

The screaming seemed to last forever. I put down the phone and cried. I moved out the week after Christmas. The pastor who married us helped with the move. He assured me that I was making the best decision for my family. He said that my husband would never change if he did not see what he was doing to his family.

I was heartbroken and depressed. My son was outraged and confused. My husband's children felt abandoned. It was the worst week of my life. I prayed to God every night for help when I couldn't sleep. This was my second marriage and I was starting to think that God was punishing me for my sins — that I didn't deserve to be happy. I felt so horrible for causing our children to suffer.

Then, my husband begged me to forgive him. He had done that before, so I said that I was only willing to go to counseling with him to see if we could salvage our marriage. He agreed to counseling, but then did something that I would never have predicted.

He called our pastor. My husband met with our pastor and told him everything. Our pastor asked him how much of the fault was his and how much of the fault was mine. My husband said that HE was at least 90 percent to blame. Our pastor told him that he had a great opportunity as a husband and father — to choose to be a HERO, or to choose to be a MONSTER. Our pastor talked to my husband for a long time. He talked to him about his role as a husband and a father and a step-father. My husband called me later to tell me about their conversation.

Then, my husband asked if we could go to church as a family. We went the Sunday after my son and I moved out. During the service, my pastor asked everyone to close their eyes (as he often does) and to raise their hands if they are willing to accept God into their lives. I was told later that my husband raised his hand.

I swear, that moment God did enter his life. He changed. I would never have believed that it was possible. I didn't have enough faith.

My son and I moved back into our house before the end of the month. I was terrified that things would go back to the way they had been. I was worried that my husband would return to his previous behavior.

But I did not need to worry, my husband had asked for God to enter his life. He really did change. It has been five months now, and we have attended church as a family every week. We have all of the same stresses now that we did before, but things are radically different. My husband is now focused on his family. He does not start weekly arguments. It seems like a miracle. I know that this happened because of God's help. I could not be more grateful.

I cannot express how different everything is now. I am joyful when I attend church, instead of tearful. I thank God for my blessings instead of begging for help. I feel so complete now because my husband, my step-children and my son all attend church services together. We still have many things to work on as a family, but I am now confident that we will succeed. I would have told you the opposite six months ago. So the lesson I have learned is to have faith. God loves you. He will answer when you call. Be patient.

Jennifer is a wife and mother in her early 40s. She and her husband have four children. Together they live in Michigan, but Jennifer works as a teacher in northern Indiana. She enjoys reading, going to her kids' soccer games and spending time with her family. Jennifer was raised Catholic, but as an adult decided to worship with her husband and children at a wonderful non-denominational Christian church.

— CHAPTER 16 —

I am Beautiful

BY GRACE J.

I met God was when I was 5 years old. I learned about Him in Sunday school and wanted to give Him my heart. I went to church and Sunday school all my life, but it was very much religion and not relationship.

In my elementary years, I would pray every night for forgiveness and salvation just in case I died that night; I wanted to be sure I was going to heaven. It felt like I had to name every sin I had done that day. As a child, this was overwhelming. I got bogged down with the dos and don'ts as I grew older. I was raised to be in church every time the doors were open, but it was just following the system.

In my teen years, I bucked and kicked under the loveless religion and system of rules of which I had no understanding. My spirit resisted the restraints put on me. I did not like to blindly follow a rule system without being able to understand the meaning/reasoning behind it. I did not know Jesus as a loving friend. I knew of heaven and hell, and of a God who had a bunch of rules that needed to be followed in order to get to heaven. But the meaning of a relationship with Jesus was lost to me. Church was boring; worship was boring; praying and reading my Bible was boring. I did not get any of it, and it was continually forced on me.

I walked away from the little I really knew of the Lord in my late teens. I felt alone and rejected. I spent the next decade trying to make heads or tails of life. I was searching for something; I just didn't know what. I was so empty and longed to be filled — I just didn't know how. I so much wanted to find love — I just didn't know where.

Through all these years I made tons of bad choices with tons of hard consequences. Along the way, some awful things happened to me. In the midst of all of that, I had reached rock bottom. I felt so worthless, so unloved, so ashamed, powerless, forgotten, unforgiven, unwanted and, most of all, rejected and abandoned by God.

The second time I met God was in my late 20s, and boy did I meet Him in a whole different way. By that time, I was sure that I had done way too much sinning to ever be loved by God. I felt I had made way too big a mess, was unforgivable and just worthless slime of the human race. I literally walked with my head hanging low and did not look people in the eyes. I had so much self-hatred. I felt like I was dead on the inside, like I was just a shell of a body walking around waiting for physical death.

But the Lord pursued me.

He lifted me up.

He forgave me and loved me.

He beckoned me.

He healed me.

He restored me.

He brought me under His wing.

And kiss by kiss, wound by wound, love by love, so gently and perfectly He put His creation back together again. I brought Him nothing but pain, hurt, shame, agony and brokenness … ashes. And He gave me beauty for it all.

He taught me about Himself, but in a whole different way. He showed me how He was so passionate for a RELATIONSHIP with me. He was so passionate about my heart, about my feelings, about my being. He showed me how He was so in love with me and longed for me to be so in love with Him; how He was concerned about my inside way more than my outside. He showed me how He wanted to chat with me … ALL DAY; just because He was so into me! (Prayer did not seem boring now!) He showed me how I moved Him when I sang to Him. (Worship did not seem boring now!) His words became fresh, new, alive and amazing! (The Bible did not seem boring now!) He showed me how being in a love relationship with Him was a moment-by-moment passionate adventure.

He showed me who He was and He showed me who I was! Both of these revelations were and continue to be life changing! And mostly He showed me how much He has and continues to pursue me. I'm forever being pursued!

I'm THAT valuable!

I'm THAT loved.

I'm THAT worth it!

He is enchanted with me, and I with Him.

His desire is for me, and mine is Him.

His eyes are on me, and mine on His.

HE BEHOLDS ME and I am beautiful!

Grace J. is passionate for the Lord and for walking in complete wholeness and freedom. She desires to help others discover the healing, captivating love of Jesus. She lives in Elkhart County with her family.

— CHAPTER 17 —

Brokenness Brings Transformational Healing

BY CAROL

The Holy Spirit recently brought 2 Corinthians 6:10 to me in light of sharing my story. There are a number of contrasts "as sorrowful, yet always rejoicing; as poor, yet making many rich; as having nothing, and yet possessing all things." I will reference this below.

I was born into a Christian home and was brought up to know the Lord. My life was centered on God and around the Bible for the most part; however, as I went into my teen years, there seemed to be a disconnect with what I was hearing and what I was living.

Let me explain: My mother was bipolar and was often "kept" in a depressive mode so that my father would be able to go to work to take care of the family. My father had a lot of health issues and was on medication. The medication (as I have learned in recent years) may have been the cause of a developing lifestyle inconsistent with God's Word.

He began having hallucinatory behavior and began asking me to spend several hours a night upstairs with him. During this time, he would share his life with me and would sexually abuse me. He also would use hypnosis on me "for the good." He felt that if I was sick, he could use that form to make me feel better. If a person was not a Christian, he could "help" them become one. These actions became a daily ritual during my high school and college days. I was unable to reason with or resist him effectively.

My life went downhill. By God's grace, I still loved the Lord and tried to follow Him in my young and undeveloped faith. But I was becoming very alone in my problem. I was trying to commit suicide, and my friendships and schooling were struggling. I confided in my pastor and my aunt. Neither of them knew how to help me. Running away from home was attempted, but there was no place to go.

As a freshman in college, the Lord brought across my path a very godly couple that took me under their wing. They nurtured my young faith and listened to my struggles. After a year, they were moving to another state and asked me to move with them. The hope was that this would bring final closure to my story at home.

My parents agreed to my move — much to my surprise! I moved and was invited to live in an apartment with two to three other godly Christian gals for the purpose of helping me grow personally in the Lord and learning to effectively share my faith around me. This was the point at which I "touched the hem of the Lord's garment." God took me out of my "poor, empty and needy state" and began transforming me into someone who, in my nothingness, was able to find "rejoicing." I began seeing God "making many rich" through me, and began realizing that I "possessed" the fullness of God inside of me.

Through godly Christian mentors and disciples, the Lord taught me the importance of "seeking God first" every day (Matthew 6:33) through a personal relationship with Him in His Word and prayer. From that training, I was taught how to practically live and share my faith (whether by life or word) with those around me. I saw God honoring my life during that move and over the next years of my life.

After about eight to 10 years of this training in many venues and through many "moves," God brought about my marriage to the "love of my youth." We had known each other in high school, dated a little before I left my home, but did not see each other for almost eight years, and re-found each other when we were 27 years old. My husband had been growing in the Lord all that time just as I had been. Our story was not a Cinderella story at the beginning, but became one as God put our two broken lives together and began bringing healing to us both.

After our marriage, we became assistant and youth pastors in Indiana. Ministry was challenging during those five years. During that time, God worked in our hearts to become missionaries in Europe for the next 15 years.

The Lord did a deep work in us and through us during our time overseas, and while there is much to share about what He did, two specific events emerged.

Many years later after the aforementioned sexual abuse, for medical reasons we returned six months early to the U.S. for our regularly scheduled furlough. During that time, my husband confronted my father about the abuse. With God's help, my dad admitted that he was wrong and acknowledged how much he had hurt me. He came to me asking for forgiveness. Because the Lord had encouraged me to forgive him many years before that, we found reconciliation. My husband and family returned to Europe and within six months, my father passed away. God gave a special "window" of opportunity by bringing us back to the U.S. earlier than planned to provide much needed emotional and spiritual healing with my dad and my past.

Also while we were in Europe, we were not prepared for what happened there. My husband and I had both operated under the understanding of what we knew, "submitting to God," but "ignoring" the devil (James 4:7). We were not taught that we needed to "resist" the devil, or even that he really existed and was "seeking to devour Christians." Being Christians, we were supposed to be immune to his work, weren't we?!

Not so! For our first years as young missionaries in Europe, we were depressed, sick, struggling in team relationships, challenged in ministry to the extreme. What we experienced did not seem normal! In Europe, we found that, in fact, Satan was alive and well on planet earth. It took two to three difficult years of stumbling around in the dark to discover help.

A friend and his wife came to help us where we lived. They explained that we were under attack from Satan who was not happy with the ministry into which we had entered. After two more years of not wanting to accept this truth, I began understanding and embracing what they were announcing to us.

My husband and I went through some personal teaching and training in that area. This began the process of getting rid of our baggage and bondage that we had been carrying around for so many years. We began learning how to put into practice James 4:7, and began learning how to help others to be personally freed up from their challenges of the past, and to submit totally to God.

Freedom and a deepened faith in Christ was more and more the result for us and for those to whom God allowed us to minister. In 1998, we moved back from Europe to the United States and, though we thought that Americans didn't have need of what we discovered abroad, our first weeks back showed us differently.

For the next 13 years and continuing back here in Indiana, God has led for us to continue in very significant ways what He led us into in

Europe. What began there as one-on-one discipleship in the areas of submitting to God daily and resisting the devil and seeing him flee, has now developed into a group format. My husband will do a 45-minute time of teaching the Word weekly on seven different areas where the enemy is allowed by many of us to have control in our lives. Then in "pair-partners," those who attend will process for themselves what God shows them as they listen to Him personally reveal His truth to them.

God has used the brokenness of our lives to bring about transformational healing, not only in us, but through us. To God be the glory!

Carol and her husband reside in the Michiana area and are actively involved in group and one-on-one discipleship training to college students and beyond. As former missionaries in Europe, they are teaching and preparing others about how to effectively minister, and to make disciples here and abroad. Carol's husband has phrased their ministry as "Preparing the Next Generation of Laborers." They have two grown children.

— CHAPTER 18 —

The Journey of Life

BY JANET

"With every decision you make I will be with you, because I am for you and not against you. The path of life is always a journey — a journey of life."

As I was out running one evening, I felt God impress upon me this simple but deep lesson. At the time I was out running on this long and winding path. It would wind to the right, and after a while it would wind to the left. On both sides of me was nothing but trees. In my mind I would find myself wondering, when will this path end? After going left I came to what looked like the end, but there was another curve winding to the right.

In my heart I knew sooner or later that I would reach my destination, and a sense of joy and accomplishment would fill my inner being. But in my mind I was fighting, fighting with fear, doubt, tiredness and anxiety, wanting this path to end — now!

Because a part of my personality is a fighter and not a quitter, I kept going, speaking to those feelings and thoughts that were running right alongside of me. I knew deep inside that with every step I was making progress, and I would sooner or later reach my destination. I must say, I wanted sooner, rather than later.

While I was out there I would run faster hoping to finish, and at times I would stop and walk looking behind me to see how far I had come. I then realized that one thing was for certain, I had to trust that this path was laid out with a purpose in mind by the one who designed it.

My experience that evening was a learned one. A part of me missed out on the joy, the fulfillment and the excitement of knowing that there was a reason for it all. I believe this was an example of what God does in our lives.

He has us on a path and we don't see the end in the natural, and if the truth be told, we don't see it clearly in the spiritual realm either. The path keeps winding. Why are there so many curves? Here is the difficult part, trusting and knowing that he will lead us, guide us and direct us down that winding path.

I must admit, some days are bright and clear and some days are so dark you can't see your way.

Remember that the Lord is our Shepherd, and when you think you've lost your way and the road keeps winding, trust that the path was laid out with a purpose in mind by the one who designed it. Remember you are growing and learning, so don't miss out on the joy that is yours. Keep moving forward, and as you look back you will see God had you all the time.

I thought to myself that evening, others had run this same route. Some had finished their course and someone else would start after I was finished. We are all faced with the same or similar questions. How? When? Where? We have many questions in this life, some have answers, and some don't. Some answers may bring you closer, and some won't. One thing I kept saying and reminding myself of — goodness and mercy shall follow me all the days of my life because He is my Shepherd.

After my run was complete, I did have a sense of joy. I did have a sense of peace and well-being, something that I regret not having fully during my run.

I know that life's journey is more than a 45-60-minute run, but some of the same principals apply. God has designed a path for me and you. The path may wind to the right. The path may wind to the left, but however long or short the path may be, I must remember my Shepherd has a plan and a destiny for me.

Later that evening sitting in my chair, I asked myself a question, "When will the journey end, and am I complete?"

Gently I heard within me a lovely voice, "There is no end in God."

There are many paths in life, and while you may come to the end of one, know that a new path begins. God is very passionate about life. That is why He created you and me. The patient love of God never ends.

So go ahead and let the path wind to the left. Let the path wind to the right. It's a journey for life with loveliness.

On this path will be people, places and things; people who will love you and some who will not; places that bring you joy and comfort and things that may bring sadness and pain. Why? I believe it is to get us closer toward our purpose; closer to love others as we love ourselves.

When we can truly love God, and love ourselves, loving others will come easy. Then we will see the path was not just for us after all.

Others will see the light that shines in you, others will need the love that flows out of you, others will need the love that flows out of you to help get them closer to their God-given purpose in this journey we call life.

Janet is a mother of two and grandmother of one from Mishawaka, Ind. She owns her own cleaning business and loves music; singing regularly for all types of functions. Janet has completed two marathons in Alaska and her third one at the age of 50 in Montana. She enjoys reading and sitting quietly in meditation talking to her Father in heaven. Janet would like to dedicate her story to her husband, Dave, who went home to be with the Lord in 2011.

— CHAPTER 19 —

Healing, Testing and Gold Teeth

BY LONDA

I was 9 years old when I accepted Jesus as my savior. I grew to be firmly committed and grounded in the word, but my relationship with God the Father was based mostly on an unhealthy fear. So I tried to be the perfect person; I didn't want Him to punish me. Jesus was someone I only knew as the one who paid for my sins, and the Holy Spirit was some mysterious part of God that I paid little attention to. That all began to change in 2002, but let me back up and tell you a bit about my journey into the most amazing and satisfying place in the Lord that I now find myself in.

Struggling With Disease

I was anemic when I was born. Then around the age of 5 I developed asthma. We lived in Northern Indiana and treatment for asthma was greatly lacking in the early 1950s. In order for me to have the best chance of outgrowing the asthma, my parents were advised by the doctor to move to a dryer climate. So they packed up my two brothers and I, and we moved to Arizona when I was 7. The asthma quickly got better, and after a few months the fevers stopped. I was only left with occasional wheezing and chest pains.

Fast-forward to my wedding day. I was 18 years old marrying my high school sweetheart. Nine months later we had our first child.

Starting around the age of 19, the asthma was traded for allergies of all kinds. I had our second daughter two-and-a-half years later. Not long after that, I began to experience strange symptoms of all kinds. They would come and go, one of them being hives whenever I would get sick and also dizzy spells and heart palpitations.

In my middle 30s I started experiencing hormonal imbalances which caused long and frequent menstrual periods, and a bad case of acne. For many years I suffered with repeated bladder infections, frequent colds, flu, asthmatic bronchitis and more.

By my late 40s I was diagnosed with hypothyroid. In addition to that, I had migraines and constant flu-like symptoms, along with all-over pain, constant head fog, extreme fatigue and chronic insomnia. I also developed irritable bowel syndrome, eczema and osteoarthritis.

I had to use a wheelchair when we went anywhere that required much walking. Our daughters had blessed us with five grandsons and the older ones thought this was great fun, but inside me I had a mounting fear that within 10 years I would be in that wheelchair permanently.

By the time I was 50 I was very ill, and for the first time in my life was becoming seriously depressed. At this point I was diagnosed with fibromyalgia; I never had a good day. The constant battle to just make it through the day was wearing me down to where I was losing hope, despairing of life and wanting God to take me home. My family was also suffering with me because there was nothing they could do to make it better. I started trying every medication that was available to help with sleep. I didn't care if I became addicted. Even with two sleeping pills a night, I was only getting two to four hours of uninterrupted sleep a night. I was truly desperate.

Introduction to Inner Healing

I began going to an upper cervical chiropractor in 2001. He turned out to be a Christian and through him I was introduced to an inner-healing-through-prayer ministry. Now, mind you, I didn't think I had any emotional problems that needed healing, but desperation will drive you to do things you normally wouldn't even entertain. I truly would have done anything that was legal to get some relief. I guess I didn't recognize depression and hopelessness as an emotional problem. Go figure!

I didn't know anyone in the area that was doing this kind of ministry, and so we sent for the training CDs and I started in. As I began listening, lightbulbs started exploding in my head! For the first time I began to have hope. If emotional healing could in any way bring some physical relief, well, I had nothing to lose and everything to gain. (Since then

I read that science has proven there is a direct connection between physical problems and long-term emotional stress in the majority of diseases.)

In inner healing the Lord speaks to areas where you have wounded emotions, and brings peace to those painful places in your history. I became addicted to the peace and was, for the first time in a long time, believing who Jesus says I am rather than who I thought I was. The more healing I got, the more I realized I needed more healing!

As I worked with my chiropractor and continued my pursuit of emotional healing with Jesus, some things in the physical got gradually better. The head fog disappeared along with the migraines. I also was able to speak more clearly without mixing up my words. The pain from the fibromyalgia greatly improved, as did my level of energy. I had all-over improvement of many symptoms and for the first time in 15 years, I felt like I was going uphill instead of downhill.

As I was walking through this physical and emotional journey, I was also seriously growing spiritually in ways I had never even considered. I became passionate for Jesus, and for the first time in my life began to experience a love relationship with my Lord. Listening to the Lord's heart for me started transforming my walk with the Lord into a depth of intimacy that I thought was only for others. Rather than just head knowledge that God loved me, I was beginning to *feel* loved by Him. It was amazing revelation for me and, oh, did I want more of that!

Testing Through Gold Teeth

Several years ago this relationship was to be tested in a very strange way. My husband and I had grown up in conservative churches and had continued in that vein all our married life. We had recently joined a church that was more in tune with the Holy Spirit. We were really hungry to see and experience the miracles we had been hearing about.

We decided to go to a Signs and Wonders conference. Well, in the middle of the conference the person speaking said to start looking for signs and wonders like gold dust, jewels and gold teeth and to ask the Lord for whatever we wanted such as healing or a specific anointing, etc.

So, to join in the fun, we started looking. I seriously, never for a moment, expected anything more than maybe a little gold dust, as I had seen that before. So you can imagine my shock when a friend of mine looked in my mouth and saw two gold molars that were not there before! I went into immediate denial! Even after about 100 people looked in my mouth, I still couldn't believe it; I was in shock!

I had no grid for this kind of miracle especially on my own person! When the speaker told us to start asking the Lord for something, I asked for healing; gold teeth were not on my list and I could not believe that God would do that to me.

The reason this was so hard for me was that, just before I was diagnosed with fibromyalgia I had gone to the elders in our church and asked them to pray for my healing. I had never seen anyone healed, but I knew it was possible because it was in the Bible. So I mustered up all the faith I could, and when they prayed for me, I fully expected to at least see improvement. Much to my dismay, over the next year I got much worse and made a vow that I would never put myself in that position again. I felt so let down and had allowed myself to be totally vulnerable with the Lord and to get worse instead of better really confirmed to me that God did not care about my suffering.

So here I was, after getting much emotional healing, willing to try it again, watching other people being healed, and I get two gold teeth instead. I have to admit I was offended. I had a severe case of TMJ and I would have much preferred to have that healed instead of getting two big gold molars! Besides, how in the world would I ever explain them!

I was shook; I felt like the Lord was being mean and almost mocking me. But I didn't stay there long because, by this time, I had gotten quite a lot of inner healing and my relationship with the Lord had been growing. So I quickly turned to Him for more healing. Even though I did not understand the why, I now understood that God is for me and not against me, and He is faithful and He loves me.

More Testing; More Healing

About a year after that incident, our relationship was to be tested again. Because of the severity of osteoarthritis in my spine I was unable to hold an adjustment for very long. When my neck would pull out I had about two days to get to my chiropractor or I would get a migraine.

One morning I was getting ready to go to him for that very reason and I heard the Lord say, "I don't want you to go."

I couldn't believe it! So I started arguing and reminding the Lord that He is the one who led me to this method of healing and what would happen if I didn't go?

All He would say to me is, "I want you to cut your ties with your chiropractor."

I began to panic; I knew that if the Lord did not heal me I would eventually slip back into full-blown symptoms. I had known this time would come when the Lord would want me to trust Him with my health, because I had an unhealthy dependency on my chiropractor and knew it would one day have to end. This was my worst nightmare; to cut off the very thing that had helped restore some quality of life, and Father was asking more than I knew how to give.

I cried and cried. Finally I texted my daughters and asked them to pray. I needed a "yes" or "no," but I did not tell them what it was about. I got a "yes" from them both, my heart sank.

That phone call to cancel my appointment was truly hard to make. I surrendered to the Lord and told Him that I would do this and if it brought Him more glory for me to be seriously sick, I would go there with Him. I did not believe that was His will though, because I had come to know Him. He is Jehovah Rapha, my God who heals me. Since that time I have not had one migraine, and my neck may pull, but it always stays in place.

Only He Can Satisfy

I have recently been diagnosed with yet another autoimmune disease, but I refuse to become offended and continue to press into the one I love, and believe all the more that He is good, merciful, kind and only He can satisfy.

Habakkuk 3:17-19 is a real place for me. I walk in a peace I never knew was possible and an excitement for the things of the Lord. I am learning to live a victorious life depending on the strength of Jesus and trusting in His faithfulness. I am learning that the reward for obedience is always greater than the cost. What started as a journey to be healed physically has turned into a passion for the healer, Jesus. He is the sign and wonder that I run after, and He never lets me down.

Oh, and by the way, the gold teeth, three years after getting them and having lots of possible explanations for them, the Lord finally shared with me the reason He gave them to me. It's just between me and the Lord for now, but I will tell you that I feel really blessed to have them.

Londa is married to her best friend, and together they have two beautiful daughters and are blessed with seven grandchildren. She and her husband are part of the pastoral team at Voice Ministries in Elkhart, Ind., where Londa is also the director of the healing ministry. Her passion is intimacy with the Lord and out of that place desires to bring others into a place of passionate pursuit of our bridegroom King Jesus Christ.

— CHAPTER 20 —

Reaching for the Bible Instead of the Bottle

BY JULIE ANN

Born in 1954 to a Czechoslovakian father and Hungarian mother, I was raised on a 100-acre farm with my older sister and younger brother. My father worked by night and farmed by day. That meant we were left with my mother a lot. She was an alcoholic.

There were lots of chores and much to do. Mom made sure we were kept busy helping her, because she was always "sick." Nothing was ever good enough for my mom. Praise didn't exist. Criticism for what we didn't do was a constant. We lived in fear. She would threaten to give us away when we didn't do what she wanted. We would literally be on our knees begging her not to give us away.

Though we were physically and mentally abused, we still sought her approval and validation. Even after winning spelling, queen and speech contests, I felt empty and unlovable. I was never able to talk to, nor trust my mother.

To make matters worse, at 8 years old I harbored a secret; my cousin had molested me. I'd been violated with no one to talk to. It left a void and confusion. I had to comfort myself as I questioned my self-worth.

On the opposite end of the spectrum, my father was kind, loving and gentle. He encouraged and supported us when he was home. But his "hands were tied" when it came to being there to protect us from her violence and abuse at night. With the stress of his life in Europe,

World War II in the army, mom's alcoholism and an undiagnosed heart condition, daddy died in his sleep at the age of 53. He met the Lord three weeks before my high school graduation. My friend, my "teddy bear," my daddy was gone. I was beyond devastated. I don't remember much of my graduation or the year of college to follow.

At 19, my life came to a standstill. A truck turned in front of a motorcycle I was a passenger on. I was thrown 75 feet into a tree, snapping my right femur in two, with multiple other injuries requiring bone and skin grafts and a rod inserted into my thigh. After one of my surgeries I stopped breathing, but God had plans for my life (Jeremiah 29:11). It was during my three-month hospital stay that God sent Susie, my nurse, to water the seed from my Catholic upbringing. I even experienced three ladies laying hands on me praying over my leg — in tongues. Freaked out, I just shut my eyes tight and waited until it was all over with.

I was sent home for six months of rehab and recovery. My sister was married and my brother was in the Air Force. I was with my mother by myself and she had sunken deeper into the bottle after daddy's death. After six months of her drunken binges, guilt trips and ongoing abuse, I crawled out of my bedroom window, never to look back. The words "I will never be like her" were on my lips.

For the next five years I lived life to the fullest, or so I thought. I was living life my way, with no regard to consequences. Alcohol had become a part of my life. I wanted to fit in somewhere. I was seeking approval, belonging and the fatherly love and affection I missed and so desperately longed for. The doctor, who had "put me back together" at 19, employed me, befriended me and later gave me what I thought was the "love" I had longed for.

Then it happened to me. I became pregnant with his child. I chose not to tell him. I didn't want to ruin his career and reputation. I terminated my employment and relationship with him. I then ran to terminate the life within me.

Alone and scared, I couldn't tell anyone. What would people think? This really wasn't a life within me — not yet. I had myself convinced. I was in denial. This couldn't be happening to me. An abortion was the answer to solve everything, or so I thought.

I was desperate. I couldn't look at myself in the mirror. I couldn't drink enough to numb my anguish and shame. I could no longer run from myself and what I was about to do.

It wasn't until I was on the abortion table, flat on my back, that I finally looked up and cried out to God, "What have I done?"

I had come face to face with reality. I could no longer deny it. I had killed the "life" within me — my baby. I went into shock and needed medical attention. I had killed my baby who I named Adam.

During the next three months God continued to tug at my heart. My heavenly Father sent people and circumstances into my life that brought me to my knees. God was calling me to the altar at a little Baptist Church. I was crying, confessing and accepting Jesus Christ as my Lord and Savior at the age of 25. I was baptized two weeks later.

Within six weeks, God's divine intervention led me to a new job. There I met my future husband, Ed. It was instant attraction. As our relationship continued, my flesh once again submitted to my need for feeling affection and special to someone.

I began to live life my way again. Alcohol became a regular part of our entertainment. Then I got a DUI. God had allowed this to happen, protecting others from harm. He also sent a dear friend to bail me out. What had I done now? It was at her house she asked me a question that hit me hard.

"Have you thought about God lately?" she asked.

I had been too busy living life my way. I slipped away from God, leaving Him out of my life. He'd been patiently waiting for me. I repented and recommitted my life to the Lord. I knew then that God hadn't, and wouldn't, leave me. He was becoming real to me — the daddy I needed.

I called Ed and told him that I had the Lord in my heart. I could no longer continue our relationship as it was. If he wanted to see me, he would find me in the little Baptist Church Sunday morning. Ed came to church. He found me there with my mother. She had seen the change in me and wanted to see what I was experiencing in a non-Catholic church. She also didn't want me to lose Ed. She liked him. After all, I was getting older!

God spoke to my mother and to Ed, above and beyond anything I had prayed for. He does that, you know. Ed, being raised a Polish Catholic, couldn't take his eyes off the pastor. The pastor spoke of how God designed a man and woman. He shared that a man should treasure his mate. The two should be equally yoked.

My mother went home amazed. Ed accepted Jesus Christ as his Lord and Savior that afternoon. He committed his life to Christ and to me. We were soon married, much to my mother's delight.

Mom was still drinking and so was I, until I became pregnant with my daughter, Heather. She was perfect; she was more precious than words could express. I didn't know I could love so deep. I drank to celebrate her birth — and continued.

Two years later my brother and mother's car was broadsided by a drunk driver. My brother's leg was badly broken and my mother had only a 1 percent chance to survive.

Between one of my mom's surgeries, I asked God to help me make amends with her and use me to lead her to Christ. Throughout my life, we fought over her selfishness and alcohol abuse. She had not been trustworthy, supportive, helpful, encouraging or very loving. But she WAS my mother, and I loved her for that.

Mom couldn't talk because of the tracheotomy in her throat. Though she listened to my every word I told her.

"Mom, we haven't always seen eye to eye, but if you can forgive me, we can forgive each other and start over. I need you and I am asking you to pray with me. I know you can't pray with your mouth, but you can pray with your heart. I want to spend eternity with you and God does too."

Her pleading eyes looked up at me from the bed as I prayed. She was praying from her heart, as I led her in the sinner's prayer. My mother was born again! I told her I loved her, as I felt the love of Christ flowing through me to her.

She whispered the words "I love you too."

As I leaned over to kiss her, one of my tears fell on her cheek. She blinked and a tear from HER eye rolled down her cheek. As our two tears rolled down her cheek, they met and became one — and continued down her face.

God answered my prayer. I had made peace with my mother after 35 years. She met the Lord six weeks later. Because of his endless love for her, he used me to bring her into the kingdom.

Then I ran to the wine to celebrate her salvation, and then to mourn her death. I was so messed up.

But I was blessed with a faithful, Christian husband, a precious daughter and soon, the son I had prayed for, named Shawn. I was born again, baptized and winning souls to Christ, yet the pull of my addiction remained and continued to get the best of me. I wasn't fooling anyone but myself.

As I selfishly isolated myself, I couldn't appreciate any of God's blessings. I could no longer hide my dependency. I became angry, irresponsible, forgetful and abusive — just like my mother.

God's divine plan of favor blessed my born-again daughter with a Godly man, whom she married; radiant and pure. My son missed her, was angry and became withdrawn. He resented me and the Alanon meetings his dad made him attend. My husband was devastated. They were all praying for me.

A breakthrough came when I was finally able to open up to someone. It was my doctor. I told her I thought I might have a problem with alcohol. It was after that confession to my doctor that I was able to confide in my brother.

"I think I'm turning out like mom," I said.

He already knew. My sister did too. I was hiding it from no one.

My brother took me to my first AA meeting. I was too ashamed to ask my husband. It was there that the reality of it hit me. I could no longer run from the truth or deny it. I was an alcoholic — just like my mother.

I attended meetings for awhile, but I knew I needed to dig deeper, to get to the source of my addiction. I wanted the desire to go away forever. I was tired of the guilt, the hiding, the shame, the humiliation and the countless times I tried to quit on my own and failed.

I knew I needed help from God. I began counseling and participating in "inner-healing" therapy at a church my brother-in-law was pastoring.

In the meantime, a yearly mammogram came back questionable. I underwent multiple testing for verification. Did I have breast cancer? I was scared. I ran to the only comfort I knew, to numb my pain and escape from reality — alcohol.

I began missing work. I lost my job. I was devastated. How would I tell my family? What had I done now?

I hurt my family. I had lost their respect and trust. Now I had lost my job and didn't know if I had cancer. I was beyond devastation. I had done this to myself. I had hit rock bottom. It was too much for me to bear. I was numb.

I couldn't wait for the next healing service at the church. I went there by myself, determined to receive my healing. I was ready to do anything to be set free from the bondage of this addiction. I found myself at the altar, completely broken, lonely and ashamed. It was at the altar that I emptied myself before the Lord. I gave Him my all; my past, my present, my future, my life. I couldn't cry hard enough, repenting from the very depth of my soul.

One by one, the Lord spoke through five people as they held me and prayed to break the chains of addiction that had me in bondage for 30 years.

The last person asked me if I had forgiven myself. What? Forgive myself? I did this TO myself! How could I?

When I was asked to repeat the words, "I choose to forgive myself," I could not get them out. It was as though Satan had his hand over my mouth. I was finally able to push the words out from deep within me. It was as though a demonic force came pouring out of my mouth. I took a deep breath and kept saying those five words over and over again until I was limp and emptied out — I was on the floor.

It was gone. God had set me free.

Later I would be so preoccupied with the anticipation of receiving my test results, I would forget to realize my desire for wine was not there. Was it really gone? Had I truly been delivered?

A week later I received positive test results; I had breast cancer.

Instead of panicking in fear, I was at peace. It was something totally new to me. I found myself reaching for the Bible instead of the bottle. I had absolutely no desire for alcohol. It was only then I realized the Lord truly had delivered me from the spirit of alcoholism.

Through my two surgeries and six weeks of radiation I was at peace. I felt God's presence as he carried me through it all. In His grip I could feel safe, loved and finally free.

During the last three years, God has been miraculously restoring love, trust and peace with my husband, son, daughter, son-in-law and even my brother and sister.

For the first time in my life, I am experiencing joy. I now have a lot to look forward to. I am willing and eager to share my story to help anyone God places in my life. Through it all I thank God for everything He has allowed in my life; to get me to where I am today. I will live for Him all the days of my life. To God be the glory!

God has blessed Julie Ann with a little cottage, nestled in a forest in Niles, Mich. It is surrounded by wildlife, fruit trees, a vegetable and flower garden and bird feeders; she has a "little piece of heaven" in her back yard. Julie Ann enjoys praise and worship music; canning and freezing produce from her garden, cooking a big meal from it and then giving thanks around her kitchen table with her husband, son, daughter and son-in-law.

— CHAPTER 21 —

From Torment to Truth

BY KELLY

I couldn't help but want to start out my story as if I was in the opening part of a movie. As I prayed and searched for what it was that I was going to write about, I determined that it's probably best that I start at the beginning.

I was sitting in a hotel room as life started taking a turn for me. I didn't know it was going to be the best turn in my life until later. Torment had become a normal part of my everyday life. This was torment that I could not seem to shake no matter what I tried.

I look back at my search and see all the things I tried. I started with transcendental meditation, even though I didn't really know what I was meditating on. I knew I was good at worrying, but there was nothing I could think of to mediate on.

Mantras were another trial by error that failed with not being able to even figure out what I wanted my mantra to be.

Lying in dark rooms letting the music take me over — well that was horrible considering the music I was listening to and the doors it was opening. I had chosen music that was satanic. I was not in the know of satanic music. At that time, I remember professing to my sister there was nothing greater or lesser than us humans. This is all there is! It wasn't long before my eyes started opening.

The path of music and meditation and opening myself up to find release only gave way for oppression and depression. It turned out in my search to find relief through my separation from my husband — who openly professed to using Satan against me, abuse and the emotional depravity — only left room for familiar spirits and lustful demons. The openness left me in a place where I no longer had control of anything, including my will in some areas.

Every area of my life was taken over — my relationships, my health, my job. As I pushed the limits of how deep in the pit I could go, I went on a trip to California for business. Fear had started to consume my thoughts, not to mention the demons that had started to touch me and keep me awake at night. No sooner had I checked into the hotel room in California, did I turn the other way and look for a way to get back to Indiana. I realized I was still being tormented, even in California. Demons started lustfully touching me again when I was in the hotel room and I had enough. I didn't know what to do, but I knew that was it. I called home to talk with my then-husband. I had told him I wanted to come home, I wanted to work on our marriage and I wanted to go to church.

Church? Really, I had no idea what I was saying. I look back now and I know that was the seed that was planted in me many years prior. Holy Spirit was already drawing me back to my real home. I returned to Indiana less than 24 hours after having arrived in California ready to make a new move in life. Fear was gripping me with tremendous strength. I returned home at sunrise on Monday morning and that very night, I was again tormented with paranoid thoughts and could not sleep.

Tuesday morning, I walked into a local church and asked to speak to a pastor. I didn't know who I was asking to come save me, but that day I asked Jesus to save me and I accepted Him as my Lord and Savior. I was handed a Bible to start reading. I would need this weapon as I had no idea what was to happen in the days to come. Something inside me had changed in a very radical way. There was a joy that I'd never experienced before. I had to know who this Jesus was.

In my decision to return back home from my business trip, I lost my job. I didn't take it as hard as I thought I would. I was telling the human resources person that I found Jesus. It didn't seem to matter that the job was over. With no work on my schedule, I had plenty of time to start re-establishing a relationship with my son, who was 3 at the time, and lots of time to read the Bible.

I was unable to listen to music for three weeks after coming to Christ as I somehow had thought something was wrong with me listening to music. I needed something and was led by Holy Spirit to pick up Nicole Nordeman's "Woven and Spun" CD, which to this day still melts my heart to listen to and feel closer to the Lord.

The torment didn't end just because I received Christ in my heart and Holy Spirit was alive in me. There was a lot to drive out. I would read my Bible at night and have evil thoughts come to mind that it was not true. So I would get out my pen and write "TRUTH" at the top of my Bible just to see it in my own writing as if I was telling myself the truth. After agonizing over all this torment, I was woken one morning by Holy Spirit to read Psalm 18:1 NLT.

I love You Lord, You are my strength.

Tears instantly filled my eyes. I then came to verse 4.

The ropes of death entangled me ...

I broke down in tears. No matter what torment, I knew that I knew that I knew, Holy Spirit was with me and Jesus saved me from everything. Not just the torment I had with demonic affliction, rape and emotional depravity, but sin, evil against me and my own wrongs. All of it was included and He was with me, forever!

To this day, that Psalm still comes to mind and still brings me to tears or expressions of great joy at the recollection of the salvation Jesus bought for me. I've continued on in my search for more of Jesus in my life. The desire to become more like Him and to prove to others He is here with us has over taken my life's purpose.

Several years back, I started teaching fitness classes. I knew the Lord had called me to the health industry, but how was I going to include my faith in classes? I continued teaching classes and building clientele while growing in my love for the Lord. My faith was and is an essence of my very being. I can't teach a class and not include the Lord. Opportunities to pray for women started opening and they were seeing changes.

There have been so many times I have seen God do things for the people attending the classes. A lady in class had a husband struggling with smoking. We prayed over a cloth that she placed under her husband's car seat. It wasn't too long before she came back to class letting me know that he was decreasing in his smoking. That right there started building my faith even more.

Shin pain was radiating up another lady's legs in the middle of class, and she stopped moving. I approached her in the middle of our routine and she allowed me to release God's presence over her. By the time I returned to the front of the class, God was already at work. She returned to her routine with us and I felt intense heat between my ankles and knees. I knew God was healing her. She left the class praising the Lord for her healing.

These are just a few experiences I have had. My most recent experience was that of choreographing a song called "Shake Heaven."

I handed everyone that walked in to class an index card. I told them to write down something in their life or someone else's life they are close to where breakthrough is needed. I told them a touch of God is needed to get over this. They had the option to write something down or not. I told them keep it near to them and when something happens, any improvement, they have the option to share what changed. Two days after we did this, a woman came to me and shared with me her testimony of what God did. Her daughter had been without a job for some time now and that day she got a job. She continued to tell me that her daughter had been on medications that were not helping her and a new prescription was given that was proving beneficial. We were able to thank Jesus as we knew He intervened.

I feel as though I have barely scratched the surface of all the amazing adventures and revelations God has to share with me, and the love that He has for His people. My walk with Him has only gotten deeper and in the worst of times, I knew He was there. In the best of times, I knew He was dancing with me. I am excited to see what happens in the next days. It's been a deep desire of mine to be totally consumed of God and I know He is raising up His people who have this desire all over the world; people who are willing to go through what it takes to throw off everything not of God.

I read through the book of Judges in awe of God's ability to possess His people. Gideon was clothed with God. Samson was powerfully overtaken by the Spirit of God in reference to Judges 14:6.

There is a hurting and dying world out there. You are a word for them. The people you come into contact with on a daily basis need the flavor of God in you. My story here only shows a brief part of almost nine years. It doesn't include the homelessness, shame, down in the pits, rejection from churches, abandoned by family members embarrassed of my circumstances.

It does, however, include a flame that burns for Jesus. If I can encourage you in your walk, it would be to pick up your lifeline of the Bible and search for what Jesus has for you. He set a flame ablaze in your heart to speak to those around you and I promise it will be worth the search.

Kelly is the owner of a dance fitness studio in South Bend, Ind. She dreamed of providing a place for people of emotional, mental and physical bondages to receive healing through self-expression and God's ability to rebuild their souls through encouragement and acceptance. God gave us the gift of dance and music to heal and bring us joy.

— CHAPTER 22 —

The Princess and the Toad

BY ISLA GRACE

Consider it pure joy, my brothers, whenever you face trials of many kinds, because you know that the testing of your faith develops perseverance. Perseverance must finish its work so that you may be mature and complete, not lacking anything. James 1:2-4

If I only knew …

Have you ever said that? Let me be more specific.

If I only knew that my knight in shining armor would turn into his father once he uttered the words "I do," I wouldn't have said them back. Or would I? I know as I tell a nutshell of my story, it is not just mine. Unfortunately, it may be yours too.

I met my knight who treated me like I was his princess. Never before had I met a man who made me feel so special and safe and understood and … you get the picture. He opened the car door for me, and he bought me thoughtful gifts and told me I was beautiful, and … well, you know. For me, it was perfect. How did I get so lucky?

We talked about marriage and were very up front with each other about things we were not willing to compromise on or change about the way we lived life. We decided we loved each other just the way we were and no changes were needed. So we had a beautiful wedding ceremony, and happily I believed I was on my way to wedded bliss. To have that rare marriage that others took notice of — the princess and the knight happily ever after. Sigh.

Two weeks after we were into our marriage, I kissed my knight and he turned into a toad. He became very judgmental and controlling. Everything I did was wrong. Sometimes he would tell me, but most of the time it was in a snicker, a roll of the eyes, put-downs in front of his friends, and then his beautiful green eyes turned into judging glares which became hard to look at. And because I couldn't do anything right and didn't do everything he told me to, I no longer deserved to be treated like a princess.

So he started to withhold from me the things that I treasured. Gone were the compliments, the gifts, the safety … and eventually the signs of his love. All of this happened within less than a year.

When I asked him what happened he replied, "We got married."

Oh … well here, let me fix that for ya! With a heavy heart I did my best to win his favor, but never seemed to gain any ground. Instead it just got worse and worse. It quickly turned into emotional abuse and I would do my best to hold my tongue, but it felt good to use it as a weapon sometimes. Of course, that didn't help any.

During this time, he started to control the things that I had told him up front about myself that I was unwilling to change. He would push and be angry about them. I would remind him of the conversation we had and how I had been totally honest. So why would you hold that against me?

"Because I thought I could change you," he replied.

Oh … well here, let me slap that thought right out of ya! Are you kidding me? What have I done? Is it too late to take back the "I do?"

I was feeling so deceived and so desperate, I could hardly function. I started to take on resentment, anger, deep hurt, a destructive thought life, victimization and loathing. I wasn't sure how I was going to make it to the rocker on the porch of old age with this toad. Being in an abusive situation, I shut down emotionally without even realizing it. I remember feeling like I was going through the motions of life without any deep emotions. Sure, I could laugh here and there, and occasionally I would cry. But nothing touched me deeply. There was no joy. It was such a low point.

Then my gracious Father in heaven had me right where He wanted me. He knew my heart was broken and I was desperate. So He set me up. A friend of mine pushed me into doing prayer counseling. I finally said I would go if it would make her feel better, even though I was totally convinced it was a waste of time. I am sure God was laughing all the way because it was such an amazing, life-changing experience I couldn't get enough! Even though it was so hard, it was so healing. It made my friend feel better, and I got my joy back! Woo hoo! I was on my way!

I started to realize that my husband wasn't born a toad, but it was through life's circumstances that had made him who he was. I started to want healing for him too, but even though he could see what it had done for me, he claimed there wasn't anything wrong with him. (I bet ya never heard that one!) So even though I was changing, my circumstances were not. I was still a target for scorn in his eyes. And even though I was still working on my healing, it was still so hard to take the abuse.

I would get really sad sometimes and feel my joy slipping away from me. I told my friend I thought I was losing my precious joy and she said, "No one can take your joy. It can't slip away from you unless you let it go."

That was a lightbulb moment! I declared right then and there that God gave me my joy and I wasn't about to let it go. It's worth fighting for! And I have it to this day!

Prayer counseling is only one way that God set me up. I was also given some Graham Cooke CDs. I remember sitting in my car listening to him talk about what he does in dealing with his persecutors.

I remember yelling at him at the top of my lungs, "Well I bet you don't *live* with your persecutor!" (Graham and I have had many conversations; he just doesn't know it yet.)

And through another one of his series, I learned a lot about making my way through the wilderness and using it to my advantage.

How do you use the wilderness to your advantage, you might ask?

It started with a simple question, "God, what do you think about me?"

Instead of letting the enemy get a foothold when my husband would say mean things to me and wonder if he was right (or think of all the horrible things I would like to retaliate with), I would ask the one I trust.

"God, right here in this moment, what do you think about that?"

The enemy never had a chance. So every time my toad was nasty, I went running to Papa and told Him all about it and let Him minister to me.

I also used it to stir me up and clean me out. When my toad would do something to make me feel hurt, I would use the skills I had learned in prayer counseling. I didn't want any lies to take root.

I have learned that I need to keep my eyes focused on the Lord no matter what is going on around me. Because as soon as I look at what is going on around me or to me, my eyes have lost their focus, and from there I can lose my footing pretty quickly.

When my focus is on my God, it is off my husband. I don't worry about how he isn't changing, how long it's taking, or how unfair it seems to be. When I keep my focus on God, He fills in the gaps of what I don't get from my husband. How fun is that? You know what else?

My goal used to be a good marriage. How shortsighted is that? Well, that is no longer the case. My goal is to walk into the arms of my Lord holding His gaze the whole way, and if I kiss my toad and he turns back into a knight someday, then that will be a bonus, but it is not my goal.

So back to the question, if I only knew, would I have said "I do?"

Absolutely.

Where else can you grow at such a warp speed? If I had wedded bliss, would I be holding tightly to the gaze of my Father? I wouldn't trade a thing to be where I am with the Lord right now. I only want to be propelled farther. It hasn't been easy to get to this point. Just like the ice skater who makes it look so easy; it takes practice. The fun thing about God is He will give you as many chances as it takes. I have learned that to gaze into my Father's eyes brings me into a relationship with Him where I find unconditional love and where I get to be a princess.

Isla Grace lives in the Michiana area with her husband and children.

— CHAPTER 23 —

Rescue Me

BY SARAH

I was never supposed to be born.

As a matter of fact, there were many people who thought I should have never been born. I was a miracle baby who survived an abortion within 24 hours.

In 1976, three years after Roe V. Wade, my mother had an IUD (intrauterine device for birth control) put in after my older sister was born. Somehow with the IUD still inside her, she conceived again and God began to knit me together. The IUD should have ended the pregnancy. but it didn't.

After a visit to the doctor, it was discovered that my mother's IUD had penetrated her uterus and was floating around by her kidneys. The doctor and his staff totally flipped out. This was unheard of. If this IUD could penetrate her uterus, a very strong muscle, it could penetrate any major organ including her spine. If I was permitted to continue growing, then the IUD could move and actually be fatal to both of us. It was determined that the pregnancy needed to be terminated immediately!

My parents, who were baby Christians at the time, believed strongly against abortion and went to seek a second opinion. The second doctor reacted the same as the first. He even went so far as to ask my father to choose which life was more important to him, this unborn fetus or his wife.

After much fear and pressure. they reluctantly scheduled an abortion for the next morning. They prepped my mother's cervix for the procedure by inserting a device that would cause her to dilate overnight so they could insert the devices needed to perform the abortion. My parents went home with a very heavy heart and a serious lack of peace.

During this whole scenario my father's cousin, also a believer who lived quite a ways away and was totally unaware of the situation, had been burdened to pray for my parents. God gave him two specific scriptures to give to my parents. That night my father's cousin called my parents. He shared with them what God told him concerning them and how God had led him to pray. These were the scriptures:

> Trust in the Lord with all your heart and lean not on your own understanding; in all your ways submit to him, and he will make your paths straight. Proverbs 3:5-6 NIV

> Children are a heritage from the Lord, offspring a reward from him. Like arrows in the hands of a warrior are children born in one's youth. Blessed is the man whose quiver is full of them. Psalm 127:3-5 NIV

After reading them, together my parents immediately knew God was speaking to them concerning this baby. My mother ran into the bathroom and removed the device.

She came running out of the bathroom holding it in her hand and bawling, "I got it out! I got it out! We are having this baby!"

The very next morning they showed up for their scheduled abortion and announced to the doctor "We are having this baby!"

This doctor was infuriated that my mother dared to take out the medical device without his permission. He yelled at them, stood up and motioned with his hands as though he were Pontius Pilate washing his hands and said, "I wash my hands of the both of you! You are going to lose your wife and your baby and we want no part of it. You are not allowed back into this hospital unless you comply with our recommendation!"

With that, my parents got up and walked out. They never did go back.

When several family members found out, they were very upset and could not understand their "crazy faith." Despite all of this, I was born at home, a healthy baby girl to a healthy mom, no complications and no abnormalities.

Fast-forward 26 years. I would once again be brought to a place where I would be completely dependant on Him for my life. I'm a newly married woman with an amazing husband. I've grown up in ministry and mission my whole life and I am passionately in love with Jesus. I've just embarked on the great adventure of marriage and now motherhood.

I am four months pregnant with my first child. I have been through a lot with my God, my best friend and my lover. We have a lot of secrets and hidden treasures between us and I love how He is with me. With one phone call came the tremors of a major shaking that would soon devastate me.

It's my mother, she says she and my father are getting a divorce. I knew there were some hiccups, but I had no idea it was this bad. It was like a wrecking ball to my chest. I don't remember much about that conversation other than that most of the time I stood with my jaw on the floor and huge tears running down my cheeks. I figured I would weather this like I had many other hardships and obstacles in my life ... not so.

This shook me to the core. Over the next few days and weeks, my relationship with God began to deteriorate into a mass of emotions, questions and angry accusations. I felt duped, like I had known God, but now realized I didn't know Him at all. I was so confused and disillusioned.

I got stuck reading the book of Job, going over and over it and getting angry at God for picking a fight with Satan over a loyal and faithful man named Job. I felt like Job. I was a good girl all my life, I did the right things and I made good decisions. But it was obvious that none of that counted for anything. Look at Job, he was a good and faithful man and God just plays a game of chess with Satan over his life and the next thing you know Job has lost everything and is sitting in a pile of ashes wearing a gunnysack! There were no guarantees! I could end up just like Job, or like my mom and dad. They sacrificed big time as pioneer pastors and gave their entire lives for the gospel only to end up losing everything (or so it seemed at the time).

God was not who I thought he was. He seemed almost schizophrenic. In one verse he says to bring all the children to him and in another he's giving orders to go and kill every living creature in a godless Amorite tribe ... even the children! Dude, make up your mind! To realize that this God you have known for so long is turning out to be something entirely different is earth shattering. I was totally stuck. I couldn't live with Him, but I couldn't live without Him either.

I told God, "If you want me back, then you're going to have to win my heart back!"

I was totally serious. I refused to pray, read my Bible, worship ... you name it ... I totally unplugged. I cried myself to sleep many nights wondering how this would all end. This is what the Bible calls the dark night of the soul. My husband would pray over me and encourage me in the night hours about God's faithfulness and His grace over me. He was my steady Eddy, never wavering or letting me wallow all alone.

This went on for about a year. This entire time I was still obligated to lead worship for the youth at our church. I felt like such a hypocrite. Leading others in worship to a God I wasn't sure I knew or even liked. How hilarious is it that some of the most anointed times of worship and ministry in our youth services came smack dab in the center of all that.

Well, God did show up and win my heart back. But not the way I thought he would.

One Sunday morning I stayed home from church alone. I sat on my couch and told God to come and pursue me, woo me, romance me, RESCUE ME! I wanted to have something, anything, a gift from God that I didn't have to earn, or be a good girl to get.

As I sat there I saw a huge cross appear before me. It was blinding and radiant and awesome! I was for a moment speechless until I realized that it was like a spotlight shining right into the deepest parts of me, illuminating EVERYTHING! I looked down at my chest and I could see inside my soul. I could see such nasty and disgusting sins and motives. My sin was so rancid and filthy it made me cringe. I couldn't believe how dirty I was. I had no idea this was all inside of me!

I was overwhelmed with the knowledge that I was completely wretched and hopeless. The cross was showing me the hidden caverns and recesses of my heart I had no idea existed. I knew without Him I was nothing, worse than nothing, scum, nasty and crusty with my sinful heart. I immediately knew I needed Him, no matter what; I couldn't live without him or His blood! I fell on my face and cried hot tears of repentance. I realized that I had needed to be rescued from myself!

I was unclean and He made me clean. I had no idea where we would start, but I knew no matter what, I could not live without Him. That day began a beautiful journey in my life to a deeper place in Christ I had never known. I had a lot of faith and security placed in my parents, my childhood memories and good godly things, but God came to shake all that away so that my trust would be in Him and Him alone!

God has rescued me three times that I know of, once from the grip of death, once from the blinding disillusionment that comes from shattered dreams and once on the cross at Calvary where He shed his blood for my sin so I could be free. I am a living testimony of the rescuing power of Jesus Christ. My God is no respecter of persons. If He rescued me, He will rescue you!

If you're wondering whatever happened with my mother and the IUD, here is how her story ends. She never went back to a doctor about her IUD, she felt led to pray and put it in Gods hands. Many years later at a church service a pastor called my mother out of the congregation and gave her a prophetic word.

"You have a foreign object in your body! I can't put my finger on it, but I know it's not supposed to be there. I am going to pray for you and God is going to remove it!"

He prayed and that was it. My mother walked back to her seat and stared at my father, shocked at what just happened. Later my mother had to go in for X-rays concerning another issue and she asked them to X-ray her abdomen, chest and groin area and see if they could see a "foreign object." They did and found NOTHING!

So, I leave you with this; God desperately desires to be close with you, He will patiently wait for you because He will not force His love on you. One day, it could be this day, you will find yourself in a place where all hope seems to be lost, and when you cry out, He will hear you and He will come to rescue you.

Sarah is living her dream with her super-hot husband on a hobby farm in Middlebury, Ind., raising her two children and her chickens. She is a passionate worshiper and musician. She and her husband have a heart to see the Kingdom of God come alive through media and the arts. She loves taking old things and making them new, just like Jesus has done with her!

— CHAPTER 24 —

Learning to be Still

BY LYDIA

In a world of distractions — TV, radio, computers, iPods, smartphones and a host of other technologies designed to constantly entertain us — I had become an expert at avoiding silence. I didn't realize it, of course, until I found myself with a problem I could not solve on my own.

You see, I'd also become quite the expert at problem solving. I was very independent and my mantra, no matter the problem, was "I can handle this on my own."

And then one day my world collapsed. Pregnant with my second child, I was having some complications and went to have everything checked out. I was shocked when the doctor told me that the pregnancy had gone wrong — it was a molar pregnancy. What I thought was a baby growing inside of me was actually a tumor.

I quickly went from being an independent woman who could handle anything to someone who couldn't even drive myself home from the doctor. My world was turned upside down. Not only was I carrying a tumor instead of a baby, the doctor told me it might be cancerous — I had to immediately prepare for surgery, undergo more tests and have ongoing treatment.

The grief of losing a baby combined with the fear of cancer added up to a problem I could not solve. At my wits end, I remembered back to my days in Catholic school and the nuns talking about a relationship with God. Having grown up Catholic and still being a practicing Catholic, I always had a dimension of faith in my life, but I never quite understood what they meant about having a relationship with God. Now I had an urgent need for Jesus to be real in my life, and I began to search for His help and His presence. I realized that He was the only one who could help me through.

In the weeks that followed, I was relieved to find out that the tumor was not cancerous, but behind the relief remained a surprising depth of loss and grief. I didn't expect to so keenly feel the loss of a baby I had never seen with my eyes or held in my arms.

It was difficult to express this grief, and I found myself struggling to deal with the loss and figure out how to move on with my life. I eventually followed the recommendation of a family member and went to see a doctor who specializes in holistic medicine, who was dedicated to helping me find healing physically, spiritually and emotionally.

During my first appointment with this doctor I had an encounter with Jesus. I had no expectation that this would be the outcome and I don't quite know how to describe it, but His presence was there — I'd never felt a more warming, loving, fatherly embrace than at that moment. The effect of this encounter caused my faith life to immediately change — I finally understood what it meant to have a relationship with Jesus and to make Him a part of my life. I finally knew how to be silent and still before God, allowing myself to feel His presence and receive His healing. I realized how the noise and distraction of my life had drawn me away from Him.

Today, I find that the calm and quiet is where I find His presence. I've learned to be still, and seek Him for answers instead of always saying "I can handle this on my own." I now know that it's better to give up control and let Him guide my life, and I have truly learned the value of His grace — it really is sufficient for me.

Lydia lives in northern Indiana with her daughter. She enjoys teaching and travelling.

— CHAPTER 25 —

Learning to Emerge

BY LINDA

I didn't realize it at the time, but it was destiny.

In the fall of 1999, just before the new millennium began, I attended Euro Summit, a Next Level International [NLI] leadership conference in Budapest, Hungary. Through a prophetic word, God called me to "come out of the shadows." No one had to tell me what that meant. I knew.

I had been working hard on the front lines of local church ministry as a senior pastor's wife and women's ministries director. However, I had made many excuses to avoid stepping outside my comfort zone, and had allowed intimidation and fear into my life. I was guilty of comparing myself to others and would always come up short in my own eyes. God said, no more! That night He offered me the grace and the courage to walk boldly in the spiritual gifts and calling on my life. He invited me into His preferred future. I said, "Yes." And my journey into this present future has been nothing short of remarkable.

God took this reluctant leader, with all my emotional baggage and set me free from the shadows smothering me. He also taught me how to use all the personal and ministry hardship I had faced to help others. Through His unique and divine plan, He gave me a platform by which to encourage and call the leadership gift out in women from many nations. It is something I would never have considered trying before.

The process began for me with a repentance of my own doubt, fear of man and pride. I was paralyzed by those sins and they were causing me to fall short of my potential and capacity. God helped me reframe how I saw myself, replacing it with His perspective of me. The truths found in Psalms 139 came alive as He put my name into those loving words. Finally, He challenged me with the words spoken by Elizabeth over Mary, the mother of Jesus.

> *Blessed is she who has believed that what the Lord has said to her will be accomplished. Luke 1:45. NIV*

It has become my life verse. He helped me understand that faith equals trust and trust is a choice. When we make the choice, the choice makes us.

It is my experience and observation that life is not kind or gentle to anyone. Our spiritual enemy is always seeking to bring destruction and death. Our human nature tries to find ways to cope, protect, ignore, medicate or run away from as much of life's pain as possible. My personal journey has included healing from a terminal illness early in life, a miscarriage, the premature birth of another child, the death of my mother from cancer, the stress of caring for my father-in-law, financial need, disloyalty, broken relationship and more. My list is not unusual, but it does reveal the various tools God has used to make me who I am today. Thankfully, there is more to my story than life's storms. My story includes victories, healings, fruitful ministry, impact, blessings, friendship, partnership and so much more.

For the past several years I have worked with NLI, a ministry training leaders across Europe since 1992. In 2002, they added the specialized area of training for women in leadership. EMERGE was birthed in my heart as I engaged with and listened to leaders across Europe, many of whom were desperate for something to change in their lives.

In 2008, the first EMERGE conference took place in Slovakia, at the very center of Europe, as a training tool to empower women. Since then it has been offered in other nations and locations. Some North American conferences have helped bridge the gap and facilitate a sisterhood of Christian leaders.

In 2010, the *www.nliemerge.com* website was launched to serve as an online community where people passionate about women in church and marketplace leadership gain encouragement, resource and training. We are glad to report that the EMERGE team of friends and supporters is growing.

It is my conviction that my story is simply a prophetic picture of God's invitation to all women everywhere. Deposited in each woman is all the potential necessary to impact nations, homes, schools and the workplace for Christ. Most women do not see themselves that way. I didn't either. But God does, and within their sphere of influence, He desires them to be all He created them to be.

Prophetic words are never guarantees of anything, but they are divine invitations that are ignited and released by willingness and obedience. I said, "Yes." And I believe for thousands of other women to say yes as well.

I continue to devote my life to challenge leaders to move to the next level, regardless of their circumstances or life stage. An international team of speakers, intercessors and trainers has come along side to make EMERGE leadership training conferences a worthwhile investment of a woman's time and resources. NLI's mission is to "Empower a whole new generation of radical leaders to equip, transform and expand the church in Europe." The EMERGE team has a vision to gather, equip and release to purpose one million women leaders over the coming decade.

My "yes" has resulted in scores of women coming out of the shadows. Now those women are daily expanding the kingdom in their places of influence, and their choice encourages others to emerge into divine destiny.

Linda is the women's development team leader of Next Level International, a dynamic mission organization empowering a new generation of radical leaders to equip, transform and expand the church in Europe. While maintaining a U.S. residence with her husband, Bill, Linda travels about 40 percent of the year, continuing to mentor and facilitate women into their God-ordained destiny. Being a wife, mother and grandmother is one of her greatest joys.

— CHAPTER 26 —

Somebody Please Love Me

BY NANCY

For most of my life I have struggled with wanting "somebody to love me for me."

My conception was not planned by my parents, but God most definitely had a plan for me from the beginning of time. The Psalmist David writes:

> *For you created my innermost being; you knit me together in my mother's womb. I praise you because I AM fearfully and wonderfully made; ... My frame was not hidden from you, I was made in the secret place, I was woven together in the depths of the earth. Your eyes saw my unformed body; all the days ordained for me were written in your book before one of them came to be. Psalm 139:13-16 NIV*

Whenever I question God's plan and purpose for my life, this is the passage He directs me back to.

My life has been much like a roller coaster in search for love and acceptance. The pursuit to somehow make sense of, and gain understanding and meaning to my life's journey has often been a painful one.

Most of my childhood memories are varying forms of abuse. The painful realization that my early days were filled with as much rejection as my adult life has not been a pleasant journey. I gave my heart to Jesus at the age of 8, and somehow I guess I figured life would be grand thereafter. Now that is from the perspective of an 8-year-old mind.

In pursuit of love and acceptance, I have discovered what love is not. Love is not sexual relationships, though one may feel a measure of love in the exchange. Love is not what I can do for you in order to gain your acceptance, to feel valued and obtain worth, though love may be expressed through an act of kindness. Love is not determined by how I am viewed by others, though one may express their affections or affirmations for me. Love "cannot" be bought, though Jesus demonstrated how much He loved me by paying an enormous price — His life — for my sin so that I can be restored to His likeness.

Love can be expressed in many ways: verbally, physically, emotionally and sexually. Abuse can also be expressed in these same manners. Many times we can get confused as to what LOVE really looks like. The people who are supposed to love you, nurture you and care for you can be the very same people who abuse you.

When you have experienced years of abuse, you think this is the norm. Anything beyond an abusive relationship looks foreign. Did I knowingly pursue abusive relationships? Absolutely not. The relationships usually started out based on what I could do to feel loved and accepted (subconsciously). Then, before long, I was feeling used and thrown away. When their need was filled, I was no longer needed. This applied in most of my relationships with family, friends and even other Christians.

Growing up on a farm I learned I could get worth from hard work. Though there was little to no affirmations given for a job well done, I took this skill with me as an adult and used it to seek out affirmations from others through my work. There were many takers and I was willing to give of my time and talents to just have a few moments of feeling loved and accepted. As I was developing into a young lady, the effects of abuse clouded my ability to make wise choices.

You may say, "Well, we have choices," and I certainly agree with you. God made us volitional beings, but when you were never given the opportunity to learn how to make choices in life, you suck at being able to discern healthy ones, especially when the innate need of man is to feel loved and accepted.

I had a distorted view of God's love for me. I thought He only loved me when I was good, when I was doing everything right, when I had everything in order (my ducks in a row). Lord forbid you move my ducks! Panic, fear and anxiety set in. Anxiety comes as a result of abuse and an inability to trust those who are supposed to make you feel safe. I believed God showed me He loved me when He blessed me, and when I wasn't being blessed I thought He had withdrawn His love for me. I was confused.

For years I viewed God as mean, controlling, manipulative, unloving, uncaring and abusive like my mother. Where most view God as being like their father, I viewed him as being like my mother. In my mind, I questioned what loving God would put a child in a home where they are not wanted and would have to endure much abuse?

We are on a journey called life. This past year has been divinely ordained by God as I've been required to reflect on past experiences, the brokenness in my life, and determine what I have learned from them. In the context of a loving and safe environment, I'm learning that it's not what I can do or have done that merits me God's love and acceptance, but it is ALL about what He has already done for me. Jesus paid the debt, the ransom, for the guilt and shame of my sin. His death at Calvary is nonreversible, it's permanent. I'm free to be ALL God created me to be because He "loves me just the way I am," the way He designed me. No one else has my DNA; He has planted His DNA in me!

The fact that we are born into a world full of sin and we have a sinful nature did not take God by surprise. What Satan meant for evil, God intends to use for His glory! My little treasure box of hurts, disappointments, fears, anxieties and assorted things that would keep me from having a loving relationship with Jesus and others, has been turned upside down and emptied. They've been exchanged for His treasures of love, forgiveness, acceptance, purpose, value and worth, patience, gentleness, kindness, longsuffering, and the list goes on.

In my weakness, He is made strong. As I entrust into God's hands those who have handed out abuse in whatever form, knowingly or unknowingly, I choose on purpose to forgive. Mark 11:25 says that if we forgive others, God will forgive us. I need God's forgiveness. I don't want anything to stand in the way of receiving God's forgiveness, neither do I desire to stand in the way of others receiving forgiveness from God. Romans 12:19 NKJV says,

Vengeance is mine, I will repay.

When I choose to let God be my vindicator, I release my right to hold you accountable.

I know that I am loved by my creator (John 3:16), and regardless of how I felt yesterday, feel today or tomorrow, His love for me never changes. There is nothing I can do to earn His love; there is nothing that would make Him withhold his love from me. I may choose to walk away from Him, but He never walks away from me. I know the Lord has a good plan for my life. His plan is to prosper me, not harm me and give me hope and a future (Jeremiah 29:11).

At times I may struggle with feeling loved, and when this happens I will speak the words of Jesus.

Get thee behind me Satan. Matthew 16:23 KJV

I have to take every thought captive that comes against what God says about me (2 Corinthians 10:5). I have to declare I am qualified to share in the inheritance of the kingdom of light because I have been rescued from the dominion of darkness and brought into His kingdom thru the redemption of Jesus Christ (Colossians 1:12-14). I have to believe I've been declared a minister of reconciliation (2 Corinthians 5:18-21).

The years of believing the lies of the enemy have been many, but today I choose, deciding on purpose as an act of my will, to declare that "God's love for ME is greater than any circumstance I will encounter, any harsh words I may hear. His love is my rock, my foundation on which I stand safe and secure!" My prayer is that:

May your unfailing love be with us Lord, even as we put our hope in you. Psalm 33:22 NIV

Nancy was born in Knox, Ind. She gave her heart to Christ at the age of 8. Though schooled in denominational/nondenominational settings, her strong belief in Christianity is not about which denomination you belong, but rather the relationship you have with Jesus Christ as your personal Lord and Savior. There is no greater relationship to have than to know Him on a personal level as my friend, my husband, my provider of all that I have need of physically, mentally, spiritually and emotionally. She is a full-time student at Bethel College studying human services/biblical studies. Her passion is to assist women in discovering healing and finding their purpose and destiny in Christ.

— CHAPTER 27 —

Life Lessons in Courage and Faith

BY GAIL

Life lessons can come at any age. My lesson in sisterhood, courage and faith happened when I was 7. My mother taught me this lesson through her example — a lesson that I carry to this day.

My mother was in an abusive relationship with my father. The abuse had been going on for years. She hid the signs of abuse from others very well — makeup, clothes to hide the scars and excuses for strange behavior.

My Head Start teacher befriended my mother. I thought that was great because I loved being in her class! She had a way of making learning fun, and she was really pretty. I never knew what they were talking about, but two years later I found out what those conversations were about. You see, that pretty teacher had the same problem that my mother had, and she told my mother that if she ever needed a place to stay, that her home was open to my mother and her daughters.

It was after my baby sister's first birthday, and I was 7. We sat in our lovely home, and sang happy birthday to her with a cupcake. I remember my mother's face. She had a look of sadness. The next day, my dad got ready for work, said goodbye and left. My mom got up and started to dress for the day. She was making breakfast, and my dad came back home for something. The truth was that he circled the block to make sure she was still home.

My father controlled everything in our lives — what we ate, wore, who called the house and who we received for company. My mother played along like everything was fine, and this time he left for work. It was around noon, and my mother waited for my father's noon phone call. He always called on his lunch break. They talked for a while, and then she hung up. I believe my father knew something was going to happen, but he didn't really know when or how.

After she hung up the phone, she told me that we were going out for a walk. We left our home with the clothes on our back, and with one diaper and a bottle for my baby sister in her purse. Little did I know that I would never see our pretty red house again.

My mother took the offer made by her new friend. This lady took us in without questions, and we stayed hidden in her house for months. My father looked everywhere for us, but his search always came up empty. Ironically, our protector lived about three-and-a-half blocks away. My mother's friend made sure that we didn't want for anything.

Finally, it was time for us to move. My mom found an apartment, and her uncle lived right across the hall from us.

After many months of hiding, my mother and father finally met face to face, and the meeting did not go well. The police had to get involved. But she came out OK. My mother faced her fears with courage, and she took a leap of faith to leave an abusive relationship.

Through my mother's faith in action, I learned that God will take care of you no matter how hopeless the situation may appear. I believe that God will put people in our paths to help us. My mother's special person also became a longtime friend. That friend showed courage, compassion and loyalty when my mother needed these qualities the most. The way she stepped up to help my mother when she fled an abusive relationship bonded these two women for life. I have tried to have those qualities in my friendships.

I believe that my mother stepped out in faith when she started walking that day; she did not know where she was going, where she would end up and what would happen to her when she arrived. She only knew that the life she was walking toward had to be better than the life that she left.

The lesson my mother taught me in faith and courage went into action when my husband became ill. I didn't know where his illness would take us, but I believed that God would see us through.

When my husband, Howard, told me that he had cancer, I was surprised. I remember sitting down in disbelief. Soon we were headed to the doctors to learn our next steps. We learned that Howard would have to have surgery to remove the cancer, and that would mean that he would lose the roof of his mouth and several teeth.

As the doctor explained this, I felt the need to excuse myself to go to the bathroom. Once I was in the restroom, I started crying, putting my hands over my mouth to muffle my sobs. I heard a knock at the door and I quickly washed my face to clear my red eyes and runny nose. I answered the door, and it was the doctor's surgical assistant. She asked if I was OK. She realized that this was a lot to take in, but she reassured me that she would be in the surgery room assisting the doctor, and that she would take good care of him. She put her arms around my shoulder and walked me back to the conference room. I made up in my mind that day that there would be no more tears. It was time to fight and I believed that it would be OK. I didn't cry anymore.

Everything went fast. Howard had surgery the next day, and he was released from the hospital two days later. Just as when my mother faced difficult times, God made sure that we were not alone. He allowed Alice to cross my mother's path during the rough time in her life. During my husband's illness and recovery, God placed people in our path who blessed us spiritually, emotionally and financially.

One day while I was in the kitchen, I just happened to notice a plaque that I had hung on the wall a year earlier. It was the poem "Footprints," and it dawned on me that during the most difficult times in my mother's life, and in my life, God carried us through. God has continued to be there for us. Today, Howard is seven years cancer free.

Thank God for life lessons in courage and faith.

Gail has been married for 20 years and is a mother of three: Chloe, 19; Howard, 16; and Katherine, 13. She works in South Bend, Ind,. as a librarian at Holy Cross School and as a health care worker at the Logan Center.

— CHAPTER 28 —

Eczema and God's Healing Through the Eyes of a Young Lady

BY MORIAH

Hello, my name is Moriah. I am 13 years old and in eighth grade.

My life changed when I got eczema. If you're wondering what eczema is, well, it's a skin condition, which causes the skin to become inflamed or irritated.

This is my journey of healing.

***

I first thought the eczema started when my family and I took a trip to Jamaica. I was about the age of 6. The water felt amazing on my skin. The air was so fresh, and I loved the sandy white beaches. I loved the way the sand kissed my skin. What I didn't like were the insects. I can still remember walking through the wooded areas of Jamaica and being itchy. I decided to ignore the itchiness, thinking it was an allergic reaction to the plants. When it was time to leave, I waved goodbye to my tropical paradise and went back to the city. I would miss it all: the food, the people and the beach.

Going back to South Bend, I felt a little melancholy. A few months after arriving back, I started getting itchy, I mean, itchier than usual. The next thing I noticed were the patches of irritated skin on my arms and shoulders. My mom thought it was an allergic reaction to our dog, so I couldn't hold our dog to my face anymore, or let him sleep in my bed. That's when the irritation moved south to the rest of my body.

My mom thought I should go to a doctor. Turns out, the doctor had no idea what it was. He recommended a dermatologist, who was supposed to be really good. My mom called him and scheduled an appointment.

The dermatologist just said, "It's an allergic reaction. There's nothing to worry about. I'll prescribe an allergy medicine and you'll be all set."

But, I wasn't all set. Not even close.

The allergy medication didn't do anything. I was still itchy and the patches became worse. They almost looked like scales. I thought it was pretty cool, me and my tomboyish self. My shorts and shirts I wore started to irritate me. My mom bought me looser shirts and skirts. Much to my distaste, she even bought dresses.

One day I was so itchy, I scratched till my skin broke open, releasing a crimson color. I cried because it hurt badly. I wanted my mom. I hopped off my bed and limped down the stairs cautiously. To my surprise, my mother was sitting on the couch talking to her friends. With tears running down my cheeks and a new wave coming, I limped in the living room. I limped to my mother and sat in her lap and cried. She asked me what was wrong and I was too much in pain to answer. She promised after she was done talking she'd give me a bath. After she was finished and all her friends left, she took me upstairs and washed me.

A few years rolled by and the patches disappeared. I was happy, I felt as free as a bird.

Then one morning when I woke up, I saw hair on my pillow. I told my parents that very same morning. Another trip to the doctor came by.

He smiled and said, "Change the shampoo you're using in her hair. Give me a call if there are any more problems."

Too bad he was wrong.

The shampoo didn't help either. I believe that the shampoo made my hair fall out more. By now, huge clumps of hair were falling out. The patches returned for another battle. They won and increased in numbers. I cried because my once really long hair was really short. It was about a couple inches long.

I was mocked in school. Do you have any idea what it's like having really long hair and then *poof* it's gone? Since my hair was long at the beginning of the year, my classmates thought I had a wig on when it suddenly became short. I stayed strong in school, not letting the hurtful things get the best of me. I kept my emotions bottled up. I know that isn't good for you, but that's how I dealt with the abuse. I wanted to punch a wall. My mom kept saying to rub my skin if it itched. The rubbing made it itch more. So instead, I slapped the itchy parts. I earned some weird looks when I was with my mom shopping. You know how I dealt with it mentally and physically, now you'll find out my relationship with God during this time.

I used to pray every night for God to heal me. At a certain point, I gave up and lost hope. When my parents took me to church, I didn't even pay attention to the message. I was so angry at God for not healing me. I questioned his power.

I would say, "God, if you're so powerful, then why won't you heal me?"

I tempted his power. I was supposed to be this good girl. How can I be this good girl if I don't even love my Father? I was sick of the teasing at school, sick of going to the doctors and them not knowing what to do and taking blood tests, the weird looks from people (well, that was more of my fault since I slapped my arms), and worse the sympathetic stares.

My family offered to cut off their hair. I found this a little strange. My brother's and dad's hair would grow back fast, while my mother, not so much. My mom offered for me to get extensions. Without hesitation, I accepted. The lady who did my extensions was a Cruella de Vil. Even though she was an evil lady, she did a pretty awesome job. I soon learned that the extensions didn't last long. They only lasted a week before they started falling out. When I was at school they fell out. I earned some laughs from my classmates. My friends protected me. They stood up for me. I guess my life was starting to look up.

I was right when I said my life started to look up. One dermatologist recommended a woman name Dr. Treadwell. She was a dermatologist who worked at Riley's Children's Hospital in Indianapolis. My family drove there and I saw kids with heartrending diseases. I was happy when the nurse called my name. I waited for the doctor in the hospital room. When she finally got here I was pretty happy. Dr. Treadwell is an African-American woman, who has short hair and a kind smile. She looked like she would take no disrespect though. She said I had a skin condition called eczema. Being my curious self, I asked what that was. She explained to me what eczema is. She also found out why I had eczema; it was because I had a zinc deficiency. Before we left, she prescribed zinc for me, which we could pick up at our Wal-Mart Pharmacy. She actually knew what I had! I left Riley with a smile on my face.

My mom heard from one of her friends of another lady who is excellent at hair. My mom took me to her house. She couldn't braid my hair because it was so short. She managed to put it in little rubber bands. I noticed my hair was starting to grow. After a few months, she was able to start braiding. We had some times when my hair wouldn't grow and sometimes when it would surprise us when it would grow a lot. I finally found a savior for my hair.

When the next year at school came, everyone was surprised how long my hair was. The teasers didn't say a word to me all year. I started praying to God again. I first apologized and I went on thanking Him. My skin started getting much better, too. With me taking the zinc, the patches got lighter and soon disappeared. I wasn't afraid to go outside anymore.

I guess I should thank eczema. The eczema strengthened my relationship with God. It also let my family meet new friends and new people. I also learned a lot about eczema.

Sometimes eczema got me out of things I didn't want to do, too. I guess everything happens for a reason. I now, thanks to God and prayer, only have eczema near my underarms, my wrists and small spots on my feet. My hair is now pretty long. Maybe the eczema will leave my wrists, feet and underarms someday. Maybe it will leave me forever. Until that day comes, I'll keep praying and believing that God will heal me.

What I would say to anybody who is going through a spiritual roller coaster is — don't stop believing in God. He's right there with you in the battle.

Moriah is 13 and lives with her family in South Bend, Ind. She loves to read and write. She also likes playing soccer for Holy Cross where she is the goalie; and running track where she is a top competitor in the shot put. Moriah hopes to have a book published on the New York Times Bestseller List someday. She is a high honors student and wants to be a doctor when she grows up.

— CHAPTER 29 —

Making Good Choices by the Grace of God

BY MYRA

By the grace of God and his mercy, I live today as a wife and mother of a teenage son and daughter, both of whom are in school and are good kids. I have been married to my college sweetheart and best friend for over 25 years and live an abundant life. I work in public service and have been there for nearly 27. I am truly blessed.

Why did my life turn out so nice? Why was I spared the life of drugs or becoming a teen mom, especially when society told me otherwise? Everything in my life from early on told me that I was not smart enough, the right skin color, or the right gender. By all accounts, my life was supposed to fail.

I was born in 1961 on the south side of Chicago. I lived in a house in a two-parent, middle-class household. I walked to school everyday and played with friends in the neighborhood. I was involved in sports and had sleepovers with friends. I later found out that my loving parents shielded me from the ugly side of life and the dangers that lurked in the world.

I later learned the reason why we lived in our neighborhood. We didn't have many choices where to live. I was unaware that Chicago was built to separate African-Americans from the rest of the city. The Dan Ryan expressway was purposely built to encapsulate blacks to remain on the southeast side of town, aka the black belt, where blacks migrated from the south for better jobs. I was oblivious to the fact that some ignorant people believed that all blacks were lazy, lived on welfare, were criminals and ruined property.

My loving parents covered my eyes and helped me to live in a Pollyanna rose-colored life; but as I got older, they were unable to shield me. I began to see so-called friends become jealous of my long hair or the attention that boys gave me. On three occasions, I was told to be in the playground after school to fight. Although I didn't grow up fighting, I found the entire seventh-grade class outside waiting for me to fight over something I didn't even remember.

I later witnessed random acts of violence such as a young guy lying on the ground in a pool of blood after he was shot in the head and later died, or a childhood friend who was stabbed to death in front of my house. His murderer was my neighbor who was a little younger than me. The blood stain from this incident lasted for at least 10 years. I would also hear about gangs in the neighborhood, where people wore different colored bandanas and flashed hand signs. If you crossed them, your future could not be promised.

I remember being afraid to go to a funeral of a really nice guy who jumped to his death off of a garage after taking LSD. We were not even in high school yet. I also had a good friend who lived down the street who became pregnant at 13. When the baby was 2 weeks old, she asked me to babysit. My mother vehemently said "no."

There were also subtle signs and signals that I was in a world where I was not included or expected to be successful: television, magazines, department store windows and billboard advertisements. All of the commercials told me that if I wasn't blond, blue-eyed, really thin and lacked skin color that I would never be what the world wanted.

The only thing I saw on TV about blacks were the repeated scenes of protesters being sprayed with water hoses, dogs being released into crowds and batons beating people on their heads. I also remember hearing about the assassination of the Rev. Dr. Martin Luther King Jr. and not being cool because my hair was too long to wear an afro.

I was chastised in high school because I didn't smoke cigarettes or marijuana. I also did not go out with any and every boy who wanted to date. Teen sex was alive and well, and some people did not know how to prevent pregnancies — or care.

One of the biggest misfortunes in my life was my so-called education. It was poor, lacked updated books and was unchallenging, and only prepared students to work at a minimum wage job or a factory. I remember my seventh-grade English teacher leaving the room each day "to go to the office." This class was free time for us! We played games, signified on each other and was even given a strip dance by a boy on the top of a desk.

I falsely thought that I was really smart in high school. I had honors math classes and got all A's without even studying. I was undefeated in my swim meets in freestyle and became a lifeguard. I was called an L-7 for speaking "proper" and being what they call today as a geek. I didn't care. I didn't want to be a thug or work at the corner candy store for life. I also had parents that would not permit it. My church was very supportive, too. My godfather was the pastor of our Lutheran congregation.

I had big dreams for my life. I expressed to my guidance counselor that I wanted to go into science. Maybe work in a laboratory. I was also interested in astronomy and car designs. However, each year I was not given any science classes such as chemistry or physics. I had three years of honors French and typing. I also refused to take calculus because I was tired of math. It was too easy! I finally took biology in my senior year. I never, ever, ever studied. What a false sense of security?

I had a rude awakening in college. I took what I thought was a simple art appreciation class, and later got my first F on a test. I couldn't believe that I got that grade after studying a little the night before. It was unthinkable. I was smart. I later took a tennis class and got a C. I didn't study for the test. It was mind-boggling that I wasn't getting all A's.

I thought about my high school years when I went to house parties with a friend who attended an expensive, highly regarded high school. The parties were at homes that had tennis courts, big swimming pools and three floors. Their parents were doctors, lawyers and judges. It was unbelievable. They were also African-American. I wanted to live like them!

When I was in my third year, I taught myself how to study with focus. I also sought help from teacher's assistants and study groups. I refused to cheat like several people in the back of various classes. I persevered and graduated.

I did it! I made it out of the "hood" with a degree in biological sciences, married a man who shared my aspirations and goals in life. Although he grew up similar to me in the neighborhood, he furthered his education by becoming a CPA and received a master's degree from the University of Chicago in business.

My husband and I, with the help of God and a supportive family, are able to provide our children with a good life. We also taught them to view themselves as smart, beautiful and confident. We didn't shield them too much about life so that they would be more prepared in the future.

So back to the questions I posed at the beginning of this story. Why did my life turn out so nice? Why was I spared the life of drugs or becoming a teen mom, especially when society told me otherwise?

Well, I believe I was spared because I did not allow other people's views or expectations to direct my path in life. I feel that life is about choices — making up your mind to set goals and accomplishing them to the best of your abilities. Life is for enjoying and sharing — by the grace of God.

Myra was born in Chicago, Ill. She was raised in a Lutheran Church. She majored in biology at Northern Illinois University. Her first and only job since college almost 27 years ago has been with the U.S. Food and Drug Administration, a scientifically based regulatory agency. She is a bioresearch specialist, whose responsibilities include inspecting human drug and medical device trials in the U.S. and Europe. She has been living in South Bend since 1996.

— CHAPTER 30 —

The Promise of Faithfulness, Strength and Love

BY CHRISTAL

On Aug. 20, 2011, I stared at my wedding ring and everything I was sure it would bring — faith of endless hopes and dreams and a lifetime of love. I sat on the edge of my bed thinking about the past six months.

I had told everyone six months prior that God has something exciting planned for my family this summer, and I couldn't wait! For months I prayed for this exciting thing. I made plans of how I thought it was going to play out based on the prophetic words that were given to me by strangers and also friends and family, and what I knew I heard the Lord say to me many times. I told my three boys to "not" be discouraged, because great things were coming!

My faith grew during this time, I opened my arms out and said come get me Lord, take all of me and whatever that means. I desire you above anything else! Nothing could kill the joy and peace that I had; I stepped out in faith and lived my life according to the promise I was sure of. I knew if I kept my eyes on My Lord everything would work out for His glory, and I was sure I knew what that was — my husband would come back to the Lord in a powerful way and that would lead to the restoration of our marriage and the healing of my family.

Now I sat and reflected on nearly two decades of our marriage.

I had married my high school sweetheart, the love of my life. He was exciting, romantic, confident and a planner. There wasn't anything he couldn't do when he set his mind to it, a true first born.

I was a true last born with a very submissive, unsure, safe, but fun to hang out with personality. He brought me to life; he centered his attention on me making me feel like everything. I could do anything with him by my side.

We married and started our family right away with the world waiting for us to conquer. I threw myself into being the best mother to our new son, while he worked hard to provide for his family. He quickly moved up the ladder, and we had two more sons. Our family was complete, and we were on top of the world.

But I felt the Lord calling me into a deeper place with Him. I started receiving inner healing and a love beyond anything I ever knew. As I watched my husband push God farther out of his life, I ran faster and tighter to His hand.

I wanted more and my husband resented me for it; anger and bitterness grew as I fell in love with the Lord and sought His best for me in every part of my life. For the first time, I had a lover that was before my husband, and now I was going to pay for it.

I felt the Lord asking me, "How far are you willing to go with me Christal? Will you love me to the end?"

I thought about that and what all of that would entail, but I knew no matter the cost, I wanted God more than my life.

I stared at my ring one more time with tears in my eye as I slipped it off and touched the place that the years had left an indent in my finger.

Who was I supposed to be now Lord? What are your plans for me? How and what do I pray for? I had spent years praying for my family, praying for healing and unity, feeling confident that that was exactly what was going to happen. All along the way I learned to keep my eyes focused on Him and to keep walking, and to not focus on what it looked like in the natural. I clung on to Him as my life spun out of control. I kept my eyes up believing for heaven to intervene.

Now four days shy of our 20th anniversary, and five weeks after my husband filed for divorce and moved out, it was finalized with the cruel words from the judge, "This court agrees that it is acceptable to dissolve this marriage."

How dare he let such a precious divine covenant be so easy to throw away? What right had he to tell me my marriage was dissolved? My heart had a hole; my body felt like it had been ripped in half it hurt so much.

Never did I think that this would happen. I don't know what tomorrow looked like.

Now I am holding on to the promises of His Word. He is my strength when I am weak, and boy do I feel week, but I also feel His strength in me. He will never leave me nor forsake me, I feel Him around me holding me up. He is my joy; I have so much joy every time I think about Him. Sometimes I walk around with a crazy smile and feel like I'm going to explode!

Everything works out for His glory and good, I know that I am a different person than I was a few years ago. I know that my sons and I are going through the fire and good is coming out of it. It is growing our faith and dependency on our Father, we are seeking Him in ways that we would have not before.

I put my ring in my jewelry box, and reach for my promise ring my husband gave me when we were 15. The Lord is telling me He can be my all if I let Him. I know now that my husband cannot complete me, the hole in my heart can only be filled by Jesus. I put the ring on my indented finger as a reminder of all the things God is to me; a promise of faithfulness, strength and love.

I think back on all of the words of healing for my family and the big exciting outcome this past summer was supposed to be. I don't understand it all, and don't want to spend too much time trying to figure it all out.

Who knows the mind of God, or how things will work out? God is perfect and I am not. I don't blame my Father for my misunderstanding of how my family will be healed or the timing of it. Or what will happen with my relationship with my now ex-husband. I just know Father wants my complete trust and that only He has my best interest intended. So I sit back and try to obey every step of the way without having to know what the steps look like.

Christal lives in northern Indiana and enjoys working at a small business. She is close with her family and gets together often for a quick coffee or a relaxing dinner. She enjoys cooking and playing games with her kids, and hanging out with her girlfriends who have been a huge support team for her. During this transition into a new life she is discovering a beauty in who she is and finding her identity in her heavenly Father and who He says she is.

— CHAPTER 31 —

Looking for Peace in All the Wrong Places

BY ALISA

It was the last day to donate coats to my sons' elementary school for a Salvation Army Project Bundle Up event. And I was determined that today those coats would make it out of my house and down to their school, with the bonus of teaching my two sons the value of giving to others.

I stuffed the coats into a plastic bag and pondered how to make sure they would remember to take them. I needed to leave for work before they left for school, and since my husband had more flexible work hours, he would be the one taking them to school, as he did every day.

But I wasn't sure I could depend on my husband to take the coats because experience had taught me that none of the "men" in my house remembered my instructions or requests, often requiring me to repeat myself to blank looks that expressed "I don't remember hearing this before."

"I am so tired of repeating myself," I grumbled as I looked around for a way to make sure they saw the bag of coats. "And, I'm tired of having to do everything myself. I've become a safety net for them. They don't even try!"

Quickly I became stressed as I tried to find a way to make sure they followed through on my instructions.

I wrote a note that shouted "Take these coats to school TODAY," and stapled it to the bag.

I took the bag first to Vincent, my 10 year old, and said, "Do you see this bag? You need to take it today to school and put it in the Project Bundle Up box. Do you understand?"

He dutifully nodded his head and continued to munch on his cereal. I turned to his younger brother, Kyle, who at 7 needed to be in constant motion in order to think and talk at the same time. As he circled the island in the kitchen emulating a chimpanzee, I tried to stop him to make sure he heard me.

As he strained against my hand I held up the bag of coats with my other hand and said, "Do you see this bag of coats? It needs to go to your school today. Please make sure that daddy takes them to your school today. Do you understand?"

He responded with his best chimpanzee shriek and continued his circular trek around the kitchen.

With the backup of the boys in place, I decided to go to one who needed to make it happen and explain to him the importance of taking the coats to their school today (not tomorrow, not next week — today). I found him shaving in the bathroom. I stood within his peripheral vision and dramatically held up the bag of coats.

"Frank, this bag of coats has to go to the kids' school today. Will you please make sure they take them? It's for the Salvation Army and today is the last day to take them."

He kept shaving and said "OK" without looking at me.

I wasn't convinced he heard me, and for the sake of clear communication, I asked him, "Will you remember, for sure, to take these coats to their school today?"

He turned and looked at me quizzically, "I heard you," he said convincingly.

"Okay," I said, as I kissed him goodbye. "Thanks for doing this, honey, I'll see you tonight."

But I still wasn't convinced they would meet this important deadline. "What else can I do," I murmured, as I eyed the clock and realized I needed to leave for work.

"Aha!" I thought. "I'll put the bag of coats with the note stapled to it in front of the door so they would have to step over it to go out the door. That way if they forgot what I said, the act of picking up the bag of coats would remind them of what I said and all would happen as it should. Other children will get the coats they need and my children will learn the value of giving. Perfect plan."

Why did I go to all this trouble which took quite a bit of time on a busy school/work morning to make sure they took a bag of coats to school? Because I was on a quest for peace.

As the wife and mother of the household, I could see clearly what needed to be done and when. I was the organizer of the schedules, the creator of the color-coded family events calendar, the memory chip of the to-do lists for everyone, and CEO of our family's busy organization. I was Command Central and I knew what it would take to make everything run smoothly.

The only problem was the family I loved and lived with didn't quite see it the same way. They counted on me, this I knew. But they didn't seem to try as hard as I did to remember and make sure things happened in order to create a smooth and peaceful atmosphere in our home. And when things didn't happen as they should, any remnant of peace I had created over an accomplished list of to-do items was shattered.

"If they just did what I asked them," I mumbled on my way to work, "things would go so much more smoothly, and I could just relax."

It seemed that the only way I could relax was if my to-do list was done and I could sit down at the end of the day with a feeling of satisfaction. But the problem was my list was never done. In fact, I often added to it as the day went on, creating a frenzied environment in which I was often frustrated and angry with my family.

"Things could be different if they just did as I asked." I thought. "But," I sighed, "at least I know the coats will make it to their school today, and that's one less thing to worry about."

Since my husband took the boys to school, I was usually the one to pick them up at the end of the day. As I drove them home, I was mulling over what needed to be done that evening and trying to figure out how to make dinner in 15 minutes or less.

Walking into the house I immediately spotted a familiar sight. Off to the side of the front door sat the bag of coats with the note I had so painstakingly written and stapled to it. As if in denial I wondered where a bag so similar to the one I had placed there this morning had came from. But quickly enough, reality set in.

I grabbed the bag, held it up high and shouted in a loud and shrill voice, "What are these coats doing here? Why didn't you take them to school?"

Looking a bit perplexed, Vince answered, "Well, when we were leaving to go to school, dad saw the bag and asked us what it was for. We didn't know so he just tossed them out of the way so we could go through the door."

I temporarily lost my mind ... and permanently lost any peace I had fashioned that day. By the time Frank got home I was in a righteous dither.

"Why didn't you take these coats to the school? I told you about them. You had to walk over them. AND IT HAD A NOTE ON IT!" Again, I was met with that perplexed look.

"I forgot," Frank said, as if this explained and absolved everything.

"You forgot?" I exclaimed. "How could you have possibly forgotten? What more can I do to make sure you and the boys do what needs to be done? To do what SHOULD be done. To HELP me! I can't do it all. I can never relax."

Then it hit me. I was looking for peace in all the wrong places.

No matter how hard I tried to control my environment and those in it to create a place to relax, I was rarely at peace. I was trying to find peace in a perfectly run household, in a completely done to-do list, in a family that would anticipate the household's needs, and meet them without prompting.

I was looking for peace in the way the world looks for it — according to my outside circumstances. I realized that even if the house was clean, the values were learned, and the snacks were made for soccer the next day, this would not produce peace in me.

Peace cannot be attained by doing things, even the right things, and does not come from a perfectly behaved family. Peace comes from Him, not them.

In John 14: 27 NIV Jesus says,

> *Peace I leave with you; my peace I give you. I do not give to you as the world gives. Do not let your hearts be troubled and do not be afraid.*

And in Philippians 4: 6-7 NIV Paul wrote,

> *Do not be anxious about anything, but in every situation, by prayer and petition, with thanksgiving, present your requests to God. And the peace of God, which transcends all understanding, will guard your hearts and your minds in Christ Jesus.*

The Greek word for peace in these scriptures is *eirene*, which means "to set at one again, quietness and rest." The meaning of "to set at one again" is basically to live harmoniously, to be able to be with one another in harmony and not strife.

Clearly I had been seeking peace in the world and not in Him. Instead of presenting my requests to God with thanksgiving, I was presenting complaints about my family with frustration. Instead of accepting His peace that is beyond my understanding, I tried to figure it out and formulize it. I needed to rest in Him, spend quiet time with Him, and accept His peace that didn't make sense to my mind. I needed to allow the peace I got from trusting Him and spending time with Him to guard my bruised heart and weary mind. I needed to just "be."

I once read a story called "A Portrait of Peace." [6] The author is unknown. It goes like this:

There was once a king who offered a prize to the artist who could paint the best picture of peace.

Many artists tried. The king looked at all the pictures. After much deliberation he was down to the last two. He had to choose between them.

One picture was a calm lake. The lake was a perfect mirror for the peaceful mountains that towered around it. Overhead fluffy white clouds floated in a blue sky. Everyone who saw this picture said that it was the perfect picture of peace.

The second picture had mountains too. These mountains were rugged and bare. Above was an angry sky from which rain fell. Lightning flashed. Down the side of the mountain tumbled a foaming waterfall. This did not appear to be a peaceful place at all.

But when the king looked closely, he saw that behind the waterfall was a tiny bush growing in the rock. Inside the bush, a mother bird had built her nest. There in the midst of the rush of angry water sat the mother bird on her nest. The king chose this picture as the perfect picture of peace.

The king chose it "Because," he explained, "peace is not only in a place where there is no noise, trouble or hard work. Peace is in the midst of things as they are, when there is calm in your heart. That is the real meaning of peace."

The peace I now desire is one in spite of my circumstances, a peace that is beyond my limited understanding, and one that allows me to respond to my family in love rather than frustration. It's a peace that only He can give.

Alisa is a former perfectionist learning to lean on and live in God's grace instead of herself; as a wife and mother of two sons, she has had lots of practice. As the product of a Christian home, Alisa totally committed herself to the Lord when she was a freshman in college; she has been pursuing a love relationship with Him ever since. In addition to her day job as the associate director of financial aid at a college, Alisa is a motivational speaker for Christian and secular venues, and designs and sells custom-made jewelry pieces and ornaments. She is very thankful for her husband, who is one of her biggest encouragers in life.

— CHAPTER 32 —

Broken-Hearted But Renewed By Him

BY JAIMEE

Above all else, guard your heart because it is the wellspring of life. Proverbs 4:23 NIV

What happens when you don't guard your heart? When you give it away to someone who doesn't deserve it? It gets beat up and broken, that's what happens.

Then we become slaves to pain that we eventually stuff deep inside. We try to move on and find someone else, hoping that time will heal, but all we do is come into another relationship wounded, disappointed and unable to fully give ourselves. It's because we've already given a part of ourselves to someone else, or in some cases, to many others.

We wonder why we can't find a mate, can't get a good guy, can't commit and can't love. We ask ourselves constantly, "What's wrong with me?"

I was one of those people.

In 2007, I was sitting in the church pew full of pain. It had been going on for nearly three years. I was tormented of images of what my life would have been like had I gotten married to "him." I would think about sweet memories and pet names we called each other. He was in my dreams. He was in my daily thoughts, and I couldn't get over it no matter how hard I tried. I would call my mom crying about it, while my then-boyfriend would be knocking at my door coming over to pick me up for a date.

"He" and I went to the same church together. Neither of us would leave the church after our breakup. Since I blamed him for the broken relationship, I told him he had to sit in the balcony. That way I could sit in our normal spot on the main floor and wallow in what could have been. He came with his new girlfriend. I occasionally brought my boyfriend, but I always looked for "him."

Secretly I hoped that he had changed. I still clung to the one percent chance that we would get back together, because Jesus answers prayer, right? Little did I know that I was asking God to stamp and fix my own agenda.

On one particular Sunday, we had an out-of-town group from Bethel Church in Redding, Calif., come and visit. I had never been this interested in a church service before in my life. Members from their ministry team were calling out words of knowledge. The last person to give a word said, "God is healing broken hearts — if you have one, stand up."

I never popped up so fast. I didn't care if "he" saw me from the balcony. I needed healing, and I was desperate. I'd cried out to God so many times in the past, but nothing changed. This time, God met me right where I was. He touched me in my heart. He healed it. I could feel His warmth in my chest; His peace in my soul.

I have to say that that moment was more than just a healing. It was a conversion of religion to relationship. I think that is the day I got saved too. I'd sat in the church pew my entire life, but always felt bound by rules. After this touch, I couldn't get enough of a new "Him" — the real "Him" — Jesus was the new "Him" for me.

The next week I found out my old love was engaged. I went home after church, prepared to eat ice cream, watch wedding movies and cry. But I never cried. Several weeks later I found out my old love was married. Again, I went home, got out my ice cream and sat on the couch waiting to cry. I couldn't even make myself cry. The wound was no longer there. It was in this instance that I knew the torment was over. The memories were still there, but there was no sadness. Instead there was hope for a future with the one God had for me.

I would soon go through a period of great pursuit of God. I would travel the country seeking His presence, wanting to know the one that changed my life, healed me and restored me.

In June of 2008, I received a prophetic word that the Lord would give me the desire of my heart in six months. I knew what that desire was — to meet my future husband.

So I believed and prepared. I went through deep cleansing of all past relationships, bringing everything to the cross. I asked the Lord to forgive me, restore what I had given away and wash my heart and mind clean. It was a process. It was emotional and even mentally draining, but the Lord sent people to encourage me and help me finish the cleansing.

Six months and two weeks later from the time I received the word, it happened to be New Year's Eve 2008. My sister and I decided to attend church that evening in Cleveland, Ohio, where I grew up.

Shortly before midnight the pastor asked everyone to come up front and pray in the New Year. We happened to stand next to two young men. Little did we know that they were best friends, who would end up being our boyfriends, and soon our fiancés and eventually our husbands.

On July 30, 2011, Nathan and I met at the altar again — this time to say our wedding vows. My prayer was that I would be fully healed of past relationships and ready to give my heart fully away on that day. Let me tell you there was some old residue and the enemy was working overtime, but the Lord is faithful. He told me I would be ready. He would finish this work. He would answer my heart's desire. And he did!

I have never been so excited about giving my heart away to another, a fully restored heart. What an honor to know the Lord would do that for me. Take what was broken, smashed to pieces and torn and make it brand new so that I could honor the man I love with my whole heart.

I can say with full confidence that there is no more torment of past relationships. There are no thoughts of "what could have been" or questions of "why?" Those past relationships are memories under the blood of Jesus.

I have also found a wonderful man that doesn't just believe in God, but seriously seeks after Him with all his heart. And my "Him," the one I fell in love with years ago. He is also Nathan's "Him" too. It is the Lord who shows Nathan how to love me the way I was created to be loved. My heart is full, my life is full and it's all because of "Him."

Jaimee is a newlywed living in Mishawaka, Ind., with her wonderful husband, Nathan. Her heart is to help others hear the voice of God, training others in the prophetic to build up the body of Christ. Currently, she works as the director of marketing and communications at Bethel College in Mishawaka, Ind. She and her husband enjoy travelling, reading books and eating good food together.

— CHAPTER 33 —
The Light of a Child
BY MELODIE

The little blue-eyed, blonde-haired boy sat quietly in the pew, head bowed, hands clasped and folded in his lap. The words "Jesus" and "amen" were barely audible from his lips. This was a very important moment in his life. Before then, he had been reluctant to allow Jesus into his heart. Then just one-and-one-half weeks later, he would go home to be with Jesus for eternity.

* * *

Izaya is my fourth grandchild and second grandson. He came into this world on Aug. 12, 2003, arms stretched out in front of him as if he were flying. He continued to 'fly' through life with his energy, creativity and enthusiasm. He was vibrant, happy and full of life. As a baby, he would normally wake up in the morning with a smile on his cherubic, dimpled face.

Izaya went into everything full-speed ahead. It was his zest for life which kept us going. He had a contagious zeal that spread to those around him. He made friends easily and had many of them — children and adults. People would comment on his beautiful smile and brilliant blue eyes that lit up a room.

Izaya loved to learn and play. He had a way of combining the two. Just about everything was fun for him. It wasn't always fun and games though. He did get into trouble quite a bit due to his impulsiveness. Our society doesn't allow for such a free spirit. It was a challenge getting him to follow the rules. With persistence and perseverance, we started to get through to him. With love and rewards, he began to understand what it meant to stay in the yard and ask permission first. He was becoming quite the young man at 5 years old.

On Thanksgiving Day, Nov. 27, 2008, my grandchildren and I made dinner to have ready when my daughter came home from work around 4 p.m. As we sat down to our meal, Izaya's friend began knocking on the door, wanting him to come out to play. I explained to him that Izaya could come out after we were finished. Impatiently, he kept knocking on the door which made Izaya eager to go play. Eventually, we let Izaya go with instructions to stay in the front yard. My daughter and I sat on the couch in front of the picture window so we could see the boys.

They were outside 15 minutes while my daughter told me how she had talked at work about how thankful she was for her four children, and her life was improving. We saw the boys running around in the front yard, and then we didn't see them for a few minutes. I mentioned that we should check on the boys. Then there was a huge BOOM! The lights went out and then flickered back on. Suddenly, there was a loud banging on the door. I opened it to see Izaya's friend, pale with eyes wide.

"Your son just blew up!" he exclaimed.

My daughter and I flew out the door and followed him. As we ran, I wondered why he was leading us to a place that was not where they should've been. Then, we saw smoke billowing out from the back of a transformer box! Without actually knowing, we knew. Our precious Izaya was dead and still burning in that box! Nothing can prepare you for the death of your child (or grandchild). Nothing compares to that kicked-in-the-gut, heart-ripped-out feeling you get when you know that your young child is gone forever and you will never get to hold him again, hear his laughter, see his smile or watch him play.

The lights literally went out for us that evening when the light of our lives was taken from us because there was no lock on a transformer box that contained 7,200 volts of electricity. The coroner said that he died instantly, which was a big comfort in an otherwise very tragic accident. We were not permitted to view his body because of severe external burns. The only explanation for this horrific tragedy was that the boys had somehow run off and saw the box unlocked and open. One of the boys had thrown a toy inside. Izaya, being the little helper that he was, went inside to get it, grabbed hold of something and was instantly electrocuted. No one knows why the lock was missing. Izaya's little friend is traumatized for life and has frequent nightmares. He had to take that year of school over again. I pray for him continually.

It is my faith in God that has helped me to survive this nightmare. The moment I knew my little buddy was gone, I wanted to be with him.

I wondered how he felt. Was he afraid? Did he feel alone? I wondered why God would take our sunshine from us. I had so many questions, but never once doubted God's ultimate wisdom in it all. I relied on Him to comfort me. I knew that although the pain of losing Izaya is great and may never go away in my lifetime; it was for the greater good.

Even in the beginning I commented, "If Izaya's death brings even one person just a little closer to God, then it is worth it." And it has.

My daughter and I have gotten closer to God. More than 500 people came to Izaya's funeral. Some were people we didn't even know and others we hadn't seen in years. In the time that has passed, I have met people from other states who heard about it and told me they were praying for our family. Prayers have been sent from all over the country!

Although I miss Izaya so very much and it is difficult to live with the void in my life, I take comfort in knowing that Jesus was there waiting with his angels to greet Izaya when he passed from this life into his eternal one. Just as comforting is knowing that I too have accepted Jesus' gift of salvation, I will see Izaya again someday and live eternally in heaven with Jesus.

At 55, Melodie is a grandmother of five. Most of her life has been spent caring for children. Not sure what she wanted to be growing up and having many interests, Melodie dabbled in different careers. She currently works for our local schools as a custodian. Since the loss of her grandson, she is reassessing her life. Melodie has decided to pursue a dream she's had for years — to write and illustrate children's books. She lives in Mishawaka, Ind.

— CHAPTER 34 —

I Have a Reason to Sing; I Have a Reason to Worship

BY ASSUMPTA

I am originally from Rwanda, Central Africa. I came to the United States in August 1990 to enroll at Southwestern Michigan College in Dowagiac, Michigan. My fiancé at the time had started attending that same school in January 1990, though we eventually transferred and graduated from Indiana University South Bend.

We came to study in the states, not only because the education was much better, but because of the ethnic conflicts taking place in the country at that time. We are both from the minority (Tutsi) ethnic group and were not allowed access to the education we wanted. There were also political tensions rising in the country, so parents who could afford to send their children abroad did so.

Some of you might remember that the situation got to its worst in 1994 when the former president (from the majority Hutu ethnicity) was in a fatal plane crush, which then provoked a long-time planned ethnic cleansing of the Tutsis. One million Tutsis was exterminated in 100 days, including both of my parents, my sister, my brother, my nephew, my grandmother, and numerous aunts, uncles, cousins, my in-laws, many friends, and neighbors.

Getting the news while so far away from home was not easy at all.

We were so helpless. At the time my twins were 6-months-old, so I had no time to grieve. On top of that, my husband and I were not born-again Christians. We ran to men for comfort, especially our fellow Rwandans . I remember crying myself to sleep, holding anger and bitterness toward anybody that was from the Hutu ethnic group, or looked like them.

It wasn't until 2001 when a preacher from Rwanda, Apostle Paul Gitwaza, held an anointed conference in Osceola, Ind. that I received Christ as my Lord and Savior. My husband joined within five months, and my family began to pursue the Lord. Little by little our healing of the heart process began to take place. We found ourselves having to deal with everyone since most of the prayer meetings were held in our own home. Through some deliverance sessions, and prayers from servants of God from Rwanda and our home church Voice Ministries, our Lord set free. Nowadays, my family celebrates walking in forgiveness, and love for all God's people regardless of their background and there is no greater peace than that. PRAISE GOD.

That same peace is helping me and my family through my current physical trial knowing that the same God who protected us while we were sinners is going to protect us now as we cry out to Him and walk in His will.

In April 2011, I started feeling some abdominal discomfort. I would always come up with an explanation; had too much starch, did not drink enough water today, you know how the Dr. Mum's opinions are!

 The pains would come on and off and many times I would lay hands on my stomach and cast the pain away and it worked. When the pains were more intense, I anointed my stomach with oil and prayed over it. Do not ask me why I never thought of a doctor's visit. Perhaps, because like many of you mothers, I had to take care of the family and minister to others, which left no time for me. It came to a point where I developed a habit of making this one sigh and then holding my stomach when the pain came. Thank God my husband noticed and insisted that I make a doctor's appointment.

I learned after some lab work, that I was slightly anemic. I argued with the doctor about how healthy my diet was, and that motivated him to order some testing. At some point they mentioned some levels of enzymes in the pancreas, called Amylase, being abnormally high. My husband and I alerted some prayer partners and by the next doctor's visit, they were surprised that somehow the levels were normal. Praise God. I felt like singing that famous African worship song in that office saying, "Oh Oh! My God Is Goodoh!"

However, the doctor kept ordering further testing until I ended up with a colonoscopy. You probably will not understand what I'm talking about if you have not been through it. Talk about a major-super cleansing of your intestines! I do not know how to describe it! I think as Christians we need that same cleansing spiritually, and often. I came to understand that as our body accumulates and retains some junk from what we eat and drink, so does our soul from what we hear, watch, read and see. Therefore, the same way our body gets weak and sick, our spiritual life also is weakened and unfruitful when our soul is mostly fed with all that junk. May the Lord help us cleanse and guard our hearts. (Proverb 4:23)

The colonoscopy revealed a tumor with cancer cells but it had not spread in any other organ. Glory be to God! I had surgery on Sept 23, 2011, from which I recovered very well. Praise God.

After a pathologist test, with the membranes surrounding where the tumor was, I found that three out of 14 lymph nodes were positive. That is the reason why the doctors recommended counteracting its spreading and reoccurrence. I started going through chemo in November. I am currently on my 11th chemo treatment — just one to go, thank God!

My Current Praise Report:

I am doing very well with the treatments. I've hardly had any side effects for a day or two. You are a faithful God. (2 Thessalonians 3:3)

At times my white and red cells would go up, which challenged the doctor because he expected the chemo to do otherwise.

I have no pain at all and am not taking any medications at all! Thank you, God for your protection. (Psalms 91: 14-16)

I have seen and heard my family getting back to prayer. My 18–year-old fasted before my chemo. I even had a testimony of a friend of our family who fasted for the first time when I started my chemo! Praise God. I prayed, "Lord, if this situation is getting people to call upon your name, I am willing to drink this cup — just increase my faith and my strength." (Matthew 14:36)

God has rebirthed a powerful prayer meeting within our Rwandese community in Michiana (Michigan-Indiana), and God has sent us His servants from Belgium and Rwanda during this time. (Psalms 133:1-3)

On one Sunday while ministering at church to one of the sisters burdened with some family circumstances, I stood in agreement with her to enjoy the holidays regardless of those circumstances. When I told her that mine would be happier despite a chemo pump, I watched God deliver her from her sorrow. Then she became concerned about me. At the end we were both thanking God for His peace that surpasses understanding. Glory be to God. (John 14:27)

I know and trust God that many more praise reports are yet to come throughout this journey. This is one of the verses I have clung on to during this time. It keeps me going.

> *And we know that in all things God works for the good of those who love Him, who have been called according to his purpose. Romans 8:28 NIV*

My thanksgiving is for God's unfailing love that I have experienced through this time. I feel His presence more tangible than ever. I thank Him for the peace He has given me and His joy which has been my strength. I am thankful for the Love He flows through my family and many friends through encouraging emails, text messages, phone calls and greeting cards ... and mostly your prayers. Thank God for all of you who committed yourselves to pray for me; those who know me and those who do not know me. Thank you so much! Remember, your labor is not in vain. (1 Corinthians 15:58)

Thank you to my church family, Voice Ministry in Elkhart, Ind.: the leaders, my brothers and sisters in the healing ministry, Watchmen on the Wall, my colleagues in the prophetic ministry, and all of you who regularly encourage me and love on me. I love you all.

To my brothers and sisters in Authentic Ministries: my spiritual father, my mentors, I love you all.

To my community in Michiana, words cannot express my gratitude towards you. Thank you for your time, the beautiful flowers, the meals, the gifts, the hugs, running errands on behalf of my family, your love. I love you all.

To all my family, friends, who flew from out of the country or out of state to spend time with me and my family, may the Lord richly reward you. To our prayer partners in South Africa, Belgium, France, Canada, England, Rwanda and many other countries, God bless you all. I declare Hebrews 6:10 over you.

I give my blessings to Joan and Jaimee who gave me and other women of God an opportunity to testify our Father's love and victory through the storm. I conclude with this chorus, words from Hillsong that plays a lot in my heart: "All of my life in every season, You are still God, I have a reason to sing, I have a reason to worship ..."

Assumpta is a mother of four; 18 year-old twins — a boy and girl, an 8 year-old and 6 year-old daughters. Today her husband works for a local high school in South Bend. She has been in full time ministry at home and in many other settings for about eight years now and feels blessed to do so. Assumpta and her husband will be celebrating their 20th year anniversary in the summer of 2012.

— CHAPTER 35 —

A Chocolate Healing — My Personal Journey From Bitterness to a Sweet Peace

BY LINDA

The interstate I was traveling on was far too familiar. Yet my heart still raced as I grew nearer to the embrace of my mother and siblings. I had to be strong! I had to be strong! Soon there would be closure and our lives could go on.

As I walked into the courtroom, I looked around the now familiar setting and saw that I was surrounded by three generations of extended family, friends and neighbors.

"These people need you to be strong," I told myself.

Soon the verdict would be read to the man who sat quietly in his chair just a few feet away; a man whose addiction to crack cocaine and alcohol had ripped away the trust, dreams and future of my family. For more than a year now we had been haunted by unbearable anxiety and fear.

"Be strong," I whispered to myself.

As each day of the trial wore on, I had studied and memorized each juror's face. The reaction in their eyes mirrored the nightmare I was privately reliving as the evidence was laid out: a package containing my father's bloodied clothes; the photographs of the bruises, the knife wounds and the bullet holes in his head.

"Hold your emotions, be strong," the voice in my head kept insisting.

Finally, the jurors all filed in. I held my breath, my chest tightened. I thought my heart would burst as each charge was read. In the ensuing silence, I was sure my pounding heart could be heard throughout the room.

Finally, a voice, "We find this man guilty as charged on all counts."

A sigh escaped my lips. Was it really over?

However, for me it wasn't over. In Mark 11:25 in the Amplified Bible we learn that the act of forgiving means to "let it drop [leave it, let it go]." I discovered I could not drop it or let it go. I had been strong for everyone but myself.

What followed were years of deep depression. During those years I found healing, but it was a gradual, painfully slow process. My emotions were so damaged that I often reacted like a wounded animal. I knew the right way to express anger was to talk to God, to tell Him what I was feeling.

"God, you said you would not put more on me than I could bear!"

"I haven't. You still have your mother," whispered a voice within me.

Yes, I still had my mother! I was reminded of the story that on the very same night my father was murdered — possibly at the same time the intruder was in their home — my mother was driving up a very steep road when suddenly her power steering malfunctioned. She called out, "In Jesus' name!" Just as her car veered to the edge of a deep mountain ravine, she miraculously regained control. The friend who was riding with her had told me later that they sat there on the side of the road for a long time discussing whether they should continue on to the church revival, or turn around and go home. The decision to continue on may very well have saved my mother's life. The very incident that delayed her return home that evening was, in fact, an act of divine intervention in disguise.

Yes, I still had my mother. "Oh taste and see that the Lord our God is good."

When asked by a news reporter how I felt about the death sentence being handed down to my father's killer, I responded, "We did not ask for it, we only prayed for justice. I will not let this destroy me; I will use it to help other people."

I had spoken from a well-meaning heart, but that heart had been crushed and needed to be sweetened before I could ever be in a place to help others.

By now you may be wondering where my chocolate healing comes into play. Let me try to explain it.

Have you ever had one of those nights when you could not sleep? In frustration, you finally get out of the bed that stubbornly refused you any comfort or rest. You walk out into the still black night, looking anxiously for the first stirring of creeping daylight. Then you hear a single note; the sweet, fresh, wide-awake note of a bird! As note answers note, you feel a glimmer of hope. Morning breaks through the darkness. The sound of a new day is in the air.

That's the feeling that came over me the day I picked up a "Prevention" magazine and began to read an article about chocolate. You see, the journey from cocoa bean to a delicious chocolate delicacy is long and difficult.

In the beginning is the cocoa tree. It grows only along the equator in the hot humid parts of Africa and South America. Attached to the trunk of the tree is a pod which is hand-picked and cut away. Inside the pod are cocoa beans. Once the beans have been dried, they are then cracked and the cocoa removed. The cocoa is then broken and crushed repeatedly until it becomes a very fine dust — the finer the dust, the higher the quality of chocolate. However, the raw cocoa is very bitter and not at all sweet. It must be blended with other ingredients to become chocolate.

As I read the article, I began to see the parallel emerging. I had been broken open and my insides had been torn out and crushed repeatedly until I no longer resembled the woman I had been. It was in this place of spiritual dust that I found myself, ready to be mixed with a new batch of ingredients that would transform me from a bitter bean into a sweet confection to be served on the master's table.

When the ancient Aztecs discovered cocoa, it was considered food for the gods and was only prepared for kings. It was mixed with spices and peppers and prepared as a bitter tea. They discovered its empowering qualities as a mood enhancer and an aphrodisiac. Who wouldn't want to overcome depression and be a better lover?

Once I realized the process that had been for years transforming me, I was able to open myself up to receive the infusion of new spices and sweeteners (and yes, a little pepper too!) that God had for me. I was experiencing a "chocolate healing" and it felt wonderful!

The Holy Spirit had been sweetening me, preparing in me something special, and a delicacy that other women crave. Out of this bitter crushing, my spirit has been released to touch the hearts of others and offer them hope in God's peace.

When my dad was murdered, a piece of his entire family died with him.

The reality is that any family can be struck down by a calamity. Facing tragedy and overcoming bitterness is not easy. However, I do know that prayer can penetrate pain, cultivating a forgiving a heart that frees you to taste the sweet healing peace of God's grace.

Whenever I savor a piece of chocolate, I am aware of the bitterness just beneath the sweetness, and I know that without the crushing, the moment of luscious flavor that delights me would not be mine. As the confection melts in my mouth, I close my eyes for just a moment and I smile.

> *Oh taste and see that the Lord is good; blessed is the woman who trusts in him. Psalm 34:8 NKJV*

Linda and her husband live in South Bend, Ind., and have been married for 48 years. Family is a top priority to them; they are proud of their son and daughter, their spouses and four beautiful grandchildren. Linda also gives honor to her 83-year-old mother who continues to minister to those addicted to life's tragic sins. Linda says, as a Titus 2 woman, she believes she has a call to minister to hurting women on a personal level. She also speaks at women's conferences, small groups and banquets.

— CHAPTER 36 —

Here I am to Worship

BY KATIE

"Conversion is stepping across a threshold into a new relationship with Jesus. We can have many conversions in our lives if we are open to the Holy Spirit." These words were spoken during a sermon given by David Ottsen, the former rector of St. Paul's Episcopal Church in Mishawaka, Ind. His words rang true for me — I have had many conversions, and this story is about a couple of them.

I am a professor at Bethel College in Mishawaka, and throughout my career I have often asked God the question, "Why am I at Bethel College?"

His reply? "Here am I to worship."

This was not the first time God gave me this answer to the same question. Right before coming to Bethel I was on a short-term mission trip to the Muslim country of Tajikistan, living with five women who did not yet know Christ. I prayed and wondered how I could reach these beautiful women with the good news of Jesus. One night I was walking with two of them, and as we were crossing over a bridge, I asked God the question, "Why am I here?"

The Lord spoke very clearly to my heart, "You are here to worship."

This was a conversion experience for me.

I was not in Tajikistan to be an evangelist to Muslims, although I was. I was not there to be an intercessor for the people of Central Asia, although I was. No, I was there for one thing — to worship God Almighty. With tears streaming down my face, I started to softly sing, "Here I am to worship, here I am to bow down, here I am to say that You're my God."

The Tajik woman next to me began to swing her arms and hum happily to herself — she was almost skipping. She had found a new freedom and new joy — and new life. Through the power of the Spirit and the love of a small band of Americans, she trusted Christ to be her Lord and Savior — and she was acting like a little child, free from fear and inhibitions. *This* was worship — watching God do miracles and set captives free. I later learned that this woman believed in Jesus after coming to one of the gatherings of the American Christians, and she saw me worshiping with tears streaming down my face. From that experience, she said she saw that Jesus was the truth. The crossing of that bridge was truly a conversion experience for me — I had crossed a threshold with Christ and knew I would never be the same.

I would like to say that when I came to Bethel in 2004, I had asked God that same question, but I did not. I knew why I was here: to teach, to profess, to be a scholar, to use the knowledge, skills and abilities I obtained in graduate school. Why ask God for his opinion? It wasn't until 2009, more than five years later, that I realized I wasn't here just for the job. I was here for Him, for Christ. He sent me here. I am not here because I earned a Ph.D. and have expertise in an area Bethel needed. No, that would mean I am in control of my life. No, I was here because God brought me here, and He brought me here to worship. I am on a mission — a mission of worship. This is not a career to me. Here I am to worship God in all I do: research, teaching, service and mentoring students. It is all worship for one whose life is cast toward God in reckless abandonment of self.

As I prepared for my tenure review in 2011, I realized it was the hand of God moving me and directing me. It was His still small voice beckoning me and guiding me. His plan? It was not to "use me" or to do some "great" work through me. No — it was to reveal me to me — to myself, and it was to reveal Himself to me as the God who is all. He is all. He is all that I need for life.

The Lord kept taking me back to the Book of First Samuel where the Israelites take the Ark of the Covenant and use it like a "good luck charm" in their battle against the Philistines. Previously, God had told them to take the Ark to battle, and they had been victorious. But this time they did not ask God, "What are your plans? Will you save us?" They simply took matters into their own hands, expecting God to act the same as he did before. They were trying to control God, to get him to line up with their plans. God would have none of it. The Ark was captured and taken into the temple of the Philistine's God, Dagan. The first night, Dagan fell on his face before the Ark. The Philistines set him back up.

The next day, once again, Dagan was on the floor, toppled over, and his hands and his head were broken off, lying on the threshold.

I have taken this as a metaphor for my life as an academic. For years as an undergraduate, I received the message, "You are what you do. Use your intellect to get ahead." The world, and sometimes the church, wants to cast us into their mold: "Use your knowledge, skills and abilities to make something of yourself. To be successful you must only think of yourself, do whatever it takes to get ahead. It is survival of the fittest. If you don't excel, you will fail and be nothing. You must publish the most, do the most. If you do not, you will be nothing. This is the only way to succeed. You are what you do." This is a something I have struggled with my whole life — the desire to be known, loved and recognized.

Yet, God says to me, "Here I am to worship." What a contrast to God's view of success:

> Do nothing out of selfish ambition or vain conceit. Rather, in humility value others above yourselves, not looking to your own interests but each of you to the interests of others. In your relationships with one another, have the same mindset as Christ Jesus. Who, being in very nature God, did not consider equality with God something to be used to his own advantage; rather, he made himself nothing by taking the very nature of a servant ... Philippians 2:3-7 NIV

He made Himself nothing. Nothing. This is sanctification — this is success. Not grasping for praise, recognition, prestige, to be first, to be right, to be known. No pride, no vain glory, no rights. Only by becoming nothing can all the fullness of Christ dwell within us. I realized this is oneness with God — by choosing nothingness Jesus reversed the choice of Adam to try and become like God. Like Dagan, I needed to have my "head" and my "hands" severed and to bow down before God. I needed to give up the identity I had built for myself from my intellect and my performance and to recognize God as the sovereign ruler of my life.

Here I am to worship.

I almost left Bethel in 2009 for the mission field because I no longer knew why I was here, and I wanted to prove to God that I loved Him — to prove my worthiness. The Lord broke my heart when He told me, "Katie, you do not need to prove your love for Me. I know you love Me. I know your heart. I want you to sit at my feet and learn from Me. You do not have to get My attention. My eyes are always on you, and you are My beloved. Only one thing is necessary. You do not have to impress Me, I already know all about you, and I love you with an infinite love. You do not have to earn My love and acceptance. I love you. I know you. You are Mine. This is your identity."

God has taught me that it is not about my plans, my visions, my strategies or my intellect. Just like the Israelites, I was relying on myself rather than on God. Why? Because I wanted to be in control of our relationship. But, when the glory of the Lord invades your temple, all you can do is fall on your face and worship before the living God. When God invades and floods your soul with Himself — all that you once relied upon: intellect, beauty, skills, knowledge, performance, the idols we use to "become like God" — are cast down and shattered. All that matters is that the living God is worshiped. God wants us — He wants our hearts. He wants me. He wants my heart, not what I can do for Him.

Here I am to worship, to bow down and place my face on the ground before God and say, "You are in control. You are God. I am nothing before You. I surrender. Do with me as Thou will."

God invites us to step across a threshold with Him and be transformed — to enter into a new relationship with Him whereby we will never be the same. May He continue his transforming work in my life, so that one day I will be entirely free of the need for praise and recognition, free of the desire to be acknowledged for my intellect and abilities, free to be His beloved child with nothing to prove and no test to pass, no grade to earn.

May the truth "I am His beloved" pervade my entire being, and may my entire life reflect the truth: "Here I am, to worship."

Katie was born in Euclid, Ohio. She was raised in the Catholic Church, but left the faith after going to a secular university and being persuaded away from Christ by atheist professors. She spent five years as an agnostic, but was led to Christ by co-workers at a national wildlife refuge in 1995. She is a conservation ecologist who loves teaching students about the biological world. She has been a professor of environmental biology at Bethel College in Mishawaka, Ind., since 2004.

— CHAPTER 37 —
The Golden Ticket
STEPHANIE

I trusted the Lord when I heard Him say a new opportunity had finally come my way. I even heard Him say it was the "golden ticket."

I had been in property management for several years. It was the first time I was offered a regional property manager position in a corporate office with a very well-known company. I have been successful in business because of hard work and the favor of the Lord, so I was excited.

I thought, "Wow, a new job opportunity, a new adventure!"

What I did not realize was the golden ticket would look much different than I expected.

After about a year into this job, I began dreading getting out of bed after I had been demoted, had a large pay cut and was transferred one hour away from home.

It hurt so bad that I could barely think about it. I would cry in my sleep from the stress of this job. I cried on my way to work and on the way home. I dreaded waking up in the morning. I drove to work and would be so scared of what was going to happen. Through the tears I hurt so deeply, feeling alone and no one could say anything to take away the embarrassment, pain and humiliation, most of which were only feelings. I know I am a strong woman and I have made it through some very difficult circumstances. Just I always believed things would work out. In this situation, I had no way out and it seemed I could do nothing to get out of it. I have never wanted to get out of something so bad in my life. I became desperate to hear the voice of the Lord.

I learned in this situation that I was broken. I had finally realized I was not in control of my life and my situation. I was after success for the wrong reasons. I was scared of losing everything and having nowhere to go and being a failure. I was pushing myself to be a full-time student and have a high position because I felt I had been going in a direction to find who I wanted to be. I felt like

I would feel good about myself because people thought, "Wow, you are a regional manager and you have a degree and you make good money ... blah, blah, blah."

My confidence was in the wrong place. I was finding my identity in trying hard for these things instead of truly knowing who I was in Christ and trusting in Him.

I realized I was trying so hard to never go back to my past, living from place to place and never really having a place of security in my life or in my family. I was pushing myself to do so much to make me feel secure and to prove I did not need anyone's help. I felt at times like I was going to die because I was so stressed from overworking myself with a 50-60-hour work week and being a full-time student, also pushing myself to do all I could in ministry.

I was unhappy in my position at work, I hated it, and I hated the things that went on in the company. People were after titles and found themselves in their work, but they were unhappy. I did not want to make work my identity.

I know that God spoke to me to take this job but it was getting harder and harder everyday to continue believing He was the one who said this job is for you. I still stood on His word and the fact that I know I heard Him say this was the golden ticket! Where was the gold, when I was being put in fire after fire and the work got harder?

I was the boss of the woman who was supposed to train me and who also wanted my position. She did not train me; she lied about me, and made me look like I was stupid. This is something I have never experienced, since I have been very successful in past positions. My trainer called me names and treated me very badly. I know now it was the enemy. I continued to believe that God would soon give justice and I did not have to worry about it. Yet, I was demoted and she took my position. I was angry, but I realized I did not even want it. This company was full of backstabbing and long hours of stress and she was miserable. The employees were more concerned about getting to the top versus being good leaders or doing what was right for the owner.

I wanted to live my life and be happy. I wanted to know what God really had for me, and if that meant losing my position, then God must have had something else for me. Waiting to get out of it was hard. I continued to pray for my leaders who hurt me through the persecution and tears.

I could not find a job that was worth leaving and God would not tell me it was time. I felt His timing was so slow. Why would He let me walk into this mess and let me lose it all and make me feel like this, when I did nothing to deserve it? I had to go to work and have a smile on my face because I had bills to pay. I felt they just wanted me to quit. If I was able to walk out I would have. I thought about doing it and that is very unlike me.

I broke down at work, I cried in front of my boss, which was the lowest point. I never let a boss see me like this. I was someone that I had never been before — WEAK. I felt so weak and broken; nothing had made me feel this broken inside. I could choose to do nothing, give up and quit or move from faith to desperation.

I thought God would have given me a way out so this would all go away, but He did not. He did not do anything until I listened and stopped focusing on, why me? I learned something from this experience. God did not allow this to happen, the enemy did this to me and I would not do anything but learn to trust in God instead of myself and stop focusing on what others thought about me. I started to let go of wanting justice and God gave me humility to still do my best. It still was hard waking up in the morning, but I found more contentment as I believed in Him. I declared, I would get back all the money taken away from me and find the right position. After the demotion, I prayed and trusted Him for one year that it would change.

Finally, during the hardest time at work, an opportunity opened for me with more money and a way out. I got a call from an employee who used to work with me and she said nothing but great things about me. She knew some of the things I went through and I interviewed with her company and got the job. It was more than I was making as a regional manager.

I was so focused on what had happened to me that all I wanted to do was prove that the negative things these people said to me were lies and I was better than that. I was so happy to give my notice and have a new job with more money than I had started with. I jumped to this new position without really listening to the Lord and what He wanted for me — I went with my feelings.

I did learn something. God taught me that we can want things so bad that He will give it to us, but it may not be His will. I say this because I started the new job and things were crazy. I realized I was out of the will of the Lord. It was not about having a new job or focusing on how much money I had to pay for things. God wanted to speak to me about my heart. God wanted real healing in my heart, healing from my past and the negative beliefs of who I thought I was and who He was to me. God wanted me to stop striving for confidence or trust in a job or anything other than Him. It was hard to trust the Lord. I have spent time with Him and listening to His truth. God has come through more than I could ever imagine.

Pushing aside this new job I only had for three months, I ran to the Lord and pressed in to find what His will was while wanting all the healing I could get. I have to say this is what I feared the most. I have always been afraid of losing my job or not being able to take care of myself. So when God showed me I had a choice, it took me those three months to pray and fast about what I should do. I never wanted to give up the money I was making and the job made me feel like I was not a failure. He never pushed me to do this and I would never suggest someone quit their job unless they had savings and or support from family. God gave me the choice — I could continue in this new job I had or I could seek out what my true identity was in Him. If I stayed in this position, I would not have had the time to be with the Lord.

During this process, God revealed to me that He loves me. It was no longer on paper, but it was in my heart. I pushed everything aside for what He was really wanting for me and He spoke. He has broken things off of me that I did not know were really in my heart. I had so much self-protection in my heart; He revealed it was a covenant I had made even as a little girl, that no one would hurt me, which kept me from even allowing the Lord's real love toward me. I was set free. I had no idea that believing no one would ever hurt me again was making this unconscious vow with myself and was really hurting me and my relationship with God.

Now I know the Lord protects me, He loves me, He provides for me and I am trusting in Him more each day. I am open to whatever He has for me. He is transforming who I was into the woman I was destined to be. It is a hard process but a great one. It takes sacrifice to really hear from the Lord and not focus on our problems. He wants true freedom from the lies the enemy tells us and then we can focus on what a wonderful loving God He is. Out of this pain and true suffering, I have started to see life does not have to be chaos and stress to be happy. God will provide for us and wants to guide us and mature us toward our true calling. He will also let us make a choice, because I know the Lord said it was my decision if I wanted to continue living a life that way or run after His peace.

What I learned about myself was a miracle. I needed to trust the Lord.

I lost who I thought I was, and now I have a new beginning. I was doing things for the wrong reasons and I was unhappy. I needed to have faith in the Lord and not in my OWN strength. I realize now that I am nothing, and all I have is because of Him, He loves me even when it hurts. I never want to go through that experience again, but the Lord taught me so much about Him and about myself through the suffering. I learned to live in faith. I gave up trying to get out of the situation, once I gave up my strength and just got up every day and trusted him for that day. He gave me enough to get through it. I learned to declare the truth over my life each day. I prayed out loud and prayed for what had been taken away from me and it came back. I know that the Lord has a purpose and a plan for my life.

Trials come and we have to have faith and trust in the Lord and do our part to still look at Him and not the situation. Yes I have complained and cried at moments — I am human; but there were days of strength when many people would have given up and called it quits. I hung onto the Lord and He provided for me. He never let me lose my job or my home. He provided more than enough. I am so thankful for the healing I have received, what He has taught me, and the transformation that is happening. The golden ticket was not a job, money or success, but finding trust, healing and the love He has for me. I found myself in Him and I am continuing this journey. Thank you, Jesus!

Stephanie is a South Bend, Ind., native. She was saved in 2005 and baptized in 2006. She has gone through transformation and is still continuing this journey. She graduated from Bethel College with her associate degree in Bible and ministry in 2011. She is still a Bethel student working toward her bachelor's degree of science in organizational management. She is involved in ministry at Christian Life Center and enjoys volunteering. She recently married a wonderful Christian man in 2012. She loves traveling, worship, spending time with friends and family, baking, photography, the beach and learning new things.

— CHAPTER 38 —

Fresh Not Plastic

BY TERRI

God has healed me and set me free in so many ways it would take an entire book to tell them all. So I will share God's mercy and grace in my near death experience, abusive upbringing in the church and suicidal moment. While painful, I can share these experiences because I am healed, delivered and free in Jesus!

A Brush with Death

When I was 9 months old, while my father was playing with me, I suddenly became paralyzed on one side of my body. I was rushed to the hospital where the doctors told my parents that I had spinal meningitis and would not live. They packed me in ice with a fever of 109 degrees and said that even if I did survive, I would be a vegetable. People began praying for me, and to the amazement of the hospital staff, my fever went away. I was released from the hospital and never had another symptom or problem ever again! God's grace and mercy had touched my life in a big way. His touch would be a common thread weaved throughout my entire life story.

An Abusive Father and Church Life

My father was a pastor and I grew up in the church, but how my father acted at church and at home were completely different. He was mentally, emotionally, physically and spiritually abusive. If that wasn't bad enough, I was also sexually abused by men in the church. This caused me to see God as someone who wanted to hurt, abuse and punish me if I did not obey all the rules in the Bible. I saw how hypocritical the people in church were; they also placed expectations upon me because I was the pastor's daughter. As I got into my teenage years, I wanted nothing to do with God or with church.

Married with Children, but Still in Pain

When I was 18, I moved out of my parents' home, got married to a wonderful man (God knew what I needed), but true intimacy was hard. Deep inside I was hurting, confused and lost, but on the outside everything looked fine. I continued to push the pain aside, not wanting to deal with it. My husband, Ron, and I had three children, but I had so many emotional issues from my past it was difficult to raise them. I would go out and leave the children with Ron and party, trying to ease the pain, but that did not work. I would eat to ease the pain, but that did not work. I would buy things and spend money we did not have to ease the pain, but that did not work either.

Coming Back Home

One day a very good friend of mine who had started going to church invited me to go with her. I decided to try it; nothing else was working and things were getting worse and worse. This church was not like any church I had been to before. They spoke about a relationship with Jesus — not rules and regulations.

A short time later, on a cold December morning, I walked down the aisle of that church and accepted God's invitation for me to come to Him. The prodigal daughter had come home. My life changed forever that day. About three weeks later, my husband also got saved, and we started on this new journey with the Lord.

I was a new creature in Christ and God had saved me, but I still had many strongholds, mindsets and lies that I believed. A friend was praying for me one day. She told me she had a vision of a vase with beautiful plastic flowers sitting on a table. Neither of us knew what this meant, but I took it as a positive thing and did not think any more about it again for many years. It would later be significant in my healing process.

A Dark Period

When I had been a Christian for about 10 years, our family went through a very difficult period. I had taken a new job, and it was very stressful. My husband had a nervous breakdown and could no longer work, we were having problems with our teenage daughter, we lost our home, and I was having some physical problems. All of this I continued to push deeper and deeper inside, always making sure everything on the outside looked OK.

I started to be confused and would forget thoughts and words while I was speaking. I wanted to sleep all the time. I could not laugh or feel happy at all. I had no idea what was happening to me and literally thought I was going crazy. The symptoms became worse, and Ron had to force me to get out of bed. Darkness surrounded me and my every thought.

One day, while at work, I sat at my desk and wrote out goodbye letters to Ron and my children. I was thinking for the last two weeks how I would commit suicide, and that day seemed like a good day to do it. I could not, and did not want to, go on living. Everything going on in my current situation and my past was pressing in on me.

I went into my boss's office (thankfully he is a Christian) and told him I was leaving for the day. He asked me where I was going. I could not tell him. He pressed for answers, as I was acting strangely, and I finally broke down and told him. He prayed for me, called Ron and then drove me to the hospital.

God Healed in Many Ways

The next year had many ups and downs, but God was so present and supplied everything I needed for the recovery process He wanted me to go through. I will say that the way God heals can be in many different ways. He chose to use many tools to help heal me as He knew what I needed and how He was going to use what I went through for His glory!

I went to a Christian counselor and began counseling. I began taking anti-depressants. I also met with some friends who had a deliverance ministry. God also put in my path a wonderful couple who had an inner-healing ministry. So many things had been pushed so far inside, and I did not want to let go of them. They were a false security for me. Jesus is gentle, kind and compassionate. He held that hurting little girl (me) in His arms. He spoke truth to the lies that I had believed for so long. Jesus set me free! While I still have a ways to go, I am certainly not the person I used to be. Writing this testimony is proof. There was a time when I was so ashamed of my past I did not want anyone to know.

I will end my testimony with this. During one of the last meetings I had with the couple for inner healing, while we were praying, Larry took a piece of paper and began to draw a picture. It was a table with a mirror behind it. On the table was a beautiful vase of flowers; you could see the reflection of the flowers in the mirror. Below the picture he wrote the words, "fresh not plastic." He had no idea about the vision my friend had about me many years earlier. God showed me that day that I had been a plastic flower with no aroma and no ability to reproduce. I was fake. But the truth now was that he had made me into a beautiful productive real flower with a sweet smell and many seeds to sow.

I can say today that I love Jesus more than anything. I no longer see Him as a God who wants to hurt, abuse and punish me like I did in my childhood years. I know now He is completely opposite. He has set me free, healed me and restored me.

I pray that what He has done in my life will encourage you and bring you to a closer, more intimate walk with Him. He loves you and died to set you free just like He did with me.

Terri was born in Waxahachie, Texas. She was raised in a charismatic church, the daughter of a pastor. She left the church in her late teens since what religion offered did not fill the emptiness. She found a true intimate relationship with Jesus after a friend invited her to church in her middle 30s. The emptiness and hopelessness had been replaced by a loving savior. She is vice president of an accounts receivables company. She lives in South Bend, Ind., and is married with three grown children and an amazing granddaughter. She has truly been blessed by God!

— CHAPTER 39 —

Tainted Blood

BY LAURA

A few months before I spent the summer in Kenya, I had adopted a little boy named Edwin through Compassion International. He was now 4 years old, and he lived just outside of Kisumu. And I, to my unbelievable joy, was going to see him.

I had packed a stuffed monkey that I brought for him, as well as a toy airplane. He had told me in a letter once that he wanted to be a pilot when he grew up. I also had paint and a picture of my family, a children's Bible, a new pair of shoes and gifts for his grandmother. A friend of mine showed up at that morning at the compound I was living in, because she wanted to come along to meet "my son."

Around 9 a.m., a woman who worked with Compassion International in Kenya, arrived with the man who would be driving us to the place where Edwin lived. We bid farewell to the other volunteers, and started off on the journey. We drove for about an hour, through the city and up into the mountains. It was a beautiful day and a beautiful drive, but I didn't enjoy the scenery as much as I normally would have — I was anxious to meet my boy.

We finally arrived at the Compassion project, and as we drove up the dirt road to park the car, children swarmed over to the fence along the edge of their school area, little hands waving frantically and beautiful smiles shining out from their dark faces. I was introduced to the project director, who then turned me around saying, "and this is Edwin."

As I turned, I saw two people: a beautiful woman in a purple dress, who I later found out was Edwin's grandmother, and standing timidly in front of her, holding both of her arms close to his face, was Edwin.

I knelt down to take his hand and he looked at me very solemnly. He was a shy little boy, and wasn't as quick to trust me as most of the other children were. He looked up at his grandmother, who was smiling from ear to ear, and then back at me, eyes full of uncertainty.

We went inside one of the buildings and met the rest of the staff and learned a little more about the Compassion project that Edwin was a part of. We talked for awhile and shortly after got back in the car to drive to Edwin's home.

Once we got in the car, I noticed that I had missed six calls from the office back in Kisumu. I thought something must have been important for them to call me so many times, so I called right back. Desmond sounded very serious, but I couldn't make out what he was saying. It sounded as though he was asking about my blood type. But that was strange — why would he be asking about that?

A few days before, we had watched a TV show that dealt with a blood transfusion, and so we had discussed our blood types. It was a miracle in itself that Desmond knew what my blood type was. But he did, and as my phone service got clearer, I could make out his voice asking, "Laura, I'm just trying to confirm your blood type. It's O+, correct?"

I wondered what had brought this subject up again, but I said, "Yeah, that's right."

There was a small silence on the phone, and then Desmond said simply, "We need you to come back to Kisumu immediately."

There was a moment of silence, and then I sat there stunned as Desmond went on to tell me that our dear friend Solomon had come to Kisumu the day before with his little 2-and-a-half-year-old son. His son was very, very sick, and had to be taken to the hospital. Today they were still in the hospital, and the little boy was quickly dying — and the hospital had no blood. They needed my blood.

My head was spinning a little as I realized the importance of this, and yet was also a little crushed to know that the visit with Edwin was to be cut so short after looking forward to it for weeks. But I knew I had to return. My prayer for this trip had been over and over again that God would use every single part of me — my hands and feet, my smile, my voice, my fingers, my words, my thoughts, my *everything*. Now He was asking for my blood.

We began the drive back to Kisumu, and I had over an hour for my mind to work over all the questions and worry about the boy and whether or not he'd live, and if we'd be too late … and I just had to remind myself that I'm not God. I'm not God.

Finally we got there, and Desmond came rushing out to meet us with bad news —

"Laura," he said. "They can't use your blood."

At the time, I was taking anti-malarial medicine. What I didn't know was that this prevented my blood from being eligible to use in a transfusion. This medicine actually had a little bit of the disease in it, so that if they used my blood, they would run the risk of injecting the boy with malaria — he would die.

This was too much — I turned my head and sank back down in the car and wept. The stress of the day and the panic of the situation had finally caught up with me, and sought escape through the tears streaming down my face. Solomon came alongside me, touched his hand to my shoulder and began to weep for his child ... I was his last hope.

We entered the hospital room to see the small boy, and as Solomon picked him up I was stunned at how sick he was. My heart ached, and I was angry — so angry — because I HAD the blood. I had the blood type he needed ... I was there ... I was ready to give him every last drop ... and because of this medicine that was tainting my blood as it coursed through my veins ... I couldn't save him.

I couldn't save him.

And as we stood there, the boy died right in front of us ... in his father's arms.

Everyone crowded around to see and to pray over them while I fought to escape, and collapsed on the railing outside. I thought I was going to be sick. Everyone told me that I needed to be strong ... that it would be alright. But I didn't want to stop crying. It hurt so much that all of this had happened ... and it hurt so much to see everyone being so strong. I almost felt as though I had to cry for every single person in that hospital — for every mother with a sick baby or a dying child who wouldn't even shed a tear, for the sake of being strong. I had to weep for their sakes.

As I stood there in that hospital, I realized — this is reality. And my heart broke.

I don't understand God. I never have. And I probably never will. What good would He be as a God if we could understand Him? But I knew that I would still praise Him — for He is good.

And as all of that happened, it made me love Kenya so much more. With such a real love — not the I-had-a-good-time-and-would-like-to-go-back love that I was accused of for so long after a short two-week trip. But a REAL love … a deep-seated passion for that place and a desire to see things happen. To see God.

After returning to the office that day after my friend's son died, I was hurting, and I was angry, and I had no idea why on earth God would have taken that young boy when I KNEW He had the power to save Him — but there came a moment when I felt God asking me, "Do you trust me?"

And with a sigh, and hands held open in helpless surrender, I said: "Yes."

Two days after the boy died was Friday, and that was the day of the funeral. I knew that after all that had happened — after feeling responsible, though I wasn't — after everything, I had to be there; for the boy, for Solomon, for myself.

But then I began to think about the children's jail that we frequently visited. This jail was full of children from age 18 down to age 6, some in there for serious crimes just as theft, rape, even murder – some just because they don't have anywhere else to go. Friday was our day to visit this jail. And I just felt such a great urgency to be there. But I kept thinking … what about the funeral? I can't abandon Solomon at this time.

But tugging at the back of my mind was the knowledge that I couldn't abandon the children at the jail, either — especially since I had just a few short weeks left in Kenya. Just then the passage of Scripture I had read for my devotions earlier the day before was brought to my mind. Jesus was calling his disciples, and one man asked to be excused to attend his father's funeral, and Jesus replied, "*Let the dead bury their dead … Follow me.*

My business is life, not death.

So I missed the funeral.

I spent the morning preparing. I knew it was right, but I had no clue what I was supposed to say to them, or why God would want me to go — almost all of the other volunteers I knew would be attending the funeral, which meant that I was basically on my own, for the first time. A friend of mine would be coming along to translate, but I was the teacher. I had no idea what God was doing … but I knew I had to follow. Step by step …

I felt as though God wanted me to talk about grace. Most of the children in that jail have never been shown anything like grace in their lives. And that was the message they needed to hear. So I began to prepare — and I paused to think how on earth I'd be able to explain to them the power of Jesus' blood to cover over all of our sins. How could they understand the power of Christ's blood to pardon the crimes they had committed, when every other day of their lives those same crimes had been pushed before their faces as the reason they were living in such a terrible situation?

And it hit me like a punch in the face: My blood, which was tainted with malaria medicine, wasn't good enough to save that boy. Because it wasn't pure, I couldn't save him. It hurt so bad that I couldn't save him.

But the beautiful picture that brought to my mind was that Christ's blood was so pure ... free from any sin or unrighteousness ... that He DID have the power to save all of mankind from an eternal death.

All the trash that I had come through the past few days was working up to this moment in God's ministry. And it was beautiful.

I told that story to the older children of the jail that day. I told them that as much as I wanted to ... I couldn't save them. But Christ could, through His perfect blood. I sang "Grace Like Rain" with them, and afterward had an unplanned altar call of sorts. I told them that if they were serious about knowing this Savior Jesus — really knowing him — to stay behind; but only if they wanted to, not because their friends were or for any other reason. This was serious.

Two or three kids stood up and looked around with slight disdain and walked out.

But 29 kids stayed behind to pray with us; 29 kids from the jail, from the smaller girls to the toughest looking boys. Friend, no matter what the circumstance, God is good.

I refuse to believe that that little boy died for nothing. I refuse to believe that God didn't see him. I knew that I had to go to that jail on that day, but I had no idea why. I also knew that God had absolutely no obligation to show me any of the reasons why. But he gave me 29 reasons why.

Laura is simply a ragamuffin in need of grace. Though raised in the church, it wasn't until visiting Africa that she began to taste the life, love and beauty that Jesus offers. Since then, she has been longing for more — and finding it. She is a wanderer by nature, thirsty for glimpses of His grace and glory in new places. Laura graduated from Bethel College in Mishawaka, Ind., in 2009 with a degree in biblical studies.

— CHAPTER 40 —

Forgiving Myself

BY LILY

As I sat on a private beach in Florida in the fall of 2000, I planned on soaking up the sun. What I didn't know that day was that my life would be changed forever. It would be just the beginning of knowing who I was in Christ, and ultimately who God had created me to be!

I won't share my entire life story, but I'll start with my early years. When I was a small girl, I had two parents that would do nearly anything for my siblings and me, and they did it time after time. I was pretty shy as a little girl and extremely sheltered. I'm not quite sure how old I was when I first realized that the outside world was not at all like the safe place my childhood home was.

We were having a party at our home one day, as we often did. That particular day not only changed me forever, but would change everything that would matter to me. I can honestly say it was the day fear made its home in my life, along with mistrust and unforgiveness. It was a summer in the late 1960s. I think I was around 5 or si6x when it happened, although it is difficult to remember when you just sweep things under the rug, like we did.

It was so exciting to get my first ride on a motorcycle with an adult family member. Everyone was getting rides and most of the other kids had already had their turn. Little did I know that what was supposed to be a fun "spin around the block," would set in motion a painfully long process of regaining stability and trust in my life.

I thought it was different that I got to sit in front of him instead of behind him like everyone else, but I was small so I just did as I was told.

Rolling out of my parent's driveway was such an exciting thing, but within minutes he started touching me. It was awful. A trusted man who was part of our extended family took advantage of me, and violated me in a way that no one should have to experience. I was so afraid, and I kept trying to pull his hand away but he seemed so strong. We kept motoring along and nothing was said for the entire ride!

I remember we ran into my mom and aunt riding bikes, so I appealed to my mom that I didn't want to ride on the motorcycle anymore. But she said I chose to ride and needed to finish. I was crushed emotionally and paralyzed physically to say anything. Once home, I told my mom right away what happened. She immediately began giving me a bath, scrubbing away and weeping all at the same time. It was so confusing! It was more than 15 years later that I learned they had confronted the situation, and the man denied it. End of story. And we were all told to stay quiet about it.

Not long after on another summer day, I was riding on the back of my brother's bike in the woods with a group of kids. The older kids rode bikes a lot faster than us younger kids, so we had been falling a bit behind.

Then out of nowhere a grown man suddenly pops into view. As the man quickly approached us, he grabbed me, yanking me off the back of the bike. I tried to hang onto my brother so tightly, but just didn't have the strength to fight out of the man's grasp. He told my brother to leave or he would kill us both. I remember that threat so clearly. As my brother rode off I began to panic, much like that other summer day on the motorcycle.

The man put me on his lap and began to kiss me very aggressively. I didn't understand what was happening, and was so scared. It wasn't long and I remember hearing the rustling of leaves and saw my little brother coming for me. He had caught up to the older kids and told them what happened. The man ran away, but the image of his face was burned in my memory for years! I remember, like before, going to my mom, and getting another vigorous bath. Years later, I realized how fortunate I was to not be kidnapped!

From that point forward, I struggled with achievement in school and making friends. I was wetting the bed every night and getting ready to enter upper elementary. My parents felt desperate and went to the "experts" for help.

In those days what the doctor said was law. Mom and Dad were told I was being rebellious, strong-willed and that I needed to be broken of this bad habit. Thinking she was given good advice, my mom began to spank me every day I woke up with a wet bed. It was so humiliating and painful and I don't remember how long it lasted, but I'll never forget the fear I felt each morning. I awoke to soaked sheets and the punishment that awaited me. It was already embarrassing, but knowing you couldn't go to an overnighter at a friend's house and risk being found out is etched in my memory.

I was held back in the fifth grade, yet didn't stop wetting the bed until the end of my sixth-grade year. Around that time, I remember the few friends I had dwindled down to one girl who was held back like me. As we walked home the first day of school, many kids were making fun of us. But she was my one friend and I clung to her very closely until we entered the seventh grade.

Kids are so fickle and mean sometimes. My only friend would soon begin telling the others I was a lesbian. I didn't even know what that meant! But I figured it must be bad. I felt so completely rejected by every girl in the school and remember my lunch routine consisting of eating alone in the cafeteria or trying to stay in the restroom stall long enough until it was time to go back to class.

The fear that gripped me in any type of relationship at school felt paralyzing. I didn't even know how to be myself. I became an easy target for those that were dealing with their own "stuff" as a teenager.

I remember at church the leaders talked about taking a mission trip to Africa, and I knew immediately I wanted to be a part. I got a job and saved every paycheck for two years except for $20 that I kept for myself. I truly believe those years taught me about discipline when it came to money. When I got back from that trip, I think part of me didn't feel like I had anything to dream for, so I began to make choices that would ultimately lead me to being a pregnant.

I delivered a beautiful healthy boy right before I turned 20. The breaking point for me was when I realized that I didn't want to be responsible for my son going to hell. I didn't want him to have the baggage or heartbreak that I was experiencing, so I thought taking him to church would fix that.

Years later I married, and not only did my husband adopt my first son, we also had three other amazing children. As our oldest entered high school and different situations happened where he would be so hurt and broken, I would feel helpless and ashamed. The pain that I caused him by the choices I made was unbearable. I would literally feel paralyzed with fear and it would consume me. It would hide itself and I would feel like I had conquered it, but something else would happen and it reminded me that it just wasn't so. You see I was not only ashamed, but literally broken for hurting the child that did nothing. I would tell him how sorry I was, but it just didn't seem to fix the pain in my heart or the reminder of what I had caused. I just couldn't forgive myself. How could I when my son continued to live in hurt and pain himself?

Over the years there were so many other occurrences and conflicts that caused me to hold onto this even more. This isn't my total tragedy, but it was the great sadness in my life.

So, it's a beautiful fall day in the year 2000, and I'm so excited to get myself adjusted on the lounge chair overlooking the ocean. I had just finished reading "What's so Amazing About Grace" by Philip Yancy, so I was enjoying the moment alone and thinking over what I had just read. Then something happened that changed my life forever. I had a vision.

Seriously, it was like watching a movie of my life starting as a small child to that very moment on the beach. I saw my story in numerous real-life vignettes. All the pain that had functionally stolen my life away passed right before me. Then God showed me a video of the life that He created for me. I was amazed by the beauty of this girl and the peaceful, fulfilled life she was living. Then suddenly I recognized the girl. It was ME. I witnessed a beautiful life no other could live but me! That day was the beginning of letting go of fear, mistrust and unforgiveness.

In 2009 I had heard about this book called "The Shack" by Paul Young. I read it on my way to Washington, DC. I couldn't put it down. It was the next part of my healing process that was already in motion. The author came to town the summer of 2011 and spoke to a small group of us at a local church. It was another one of those days that changed my life forever.

As Paul shared so openly, I felt an uncontrollable emotion and I felt like if I began to weep I would never stop. I kept sipping away on my soda just to fight back the emotions as we sat there. My husband and I eventually went out to the car and we both began to sob. There was one point he looked at me in the car and said, "You need to forgive yourself."

You see I had forgiven everyone but me! That day on the beach in 2000, God did an amazing work in my life, but it took another 11 years to truly forgive me. I had the opportunity to meet Paul and asked him about this. He said the biggest and final part is always forgiving yourself. I have days where I might feel the pain that my son is going thru, but it has no place of ownership in my life.

And by the way, the video that God showed me back in 2000 is indeed my life now. It feels like life has just begun!

Lily lives in South Bend, Ind., with her husband and four boys. She enjoys traveling and loves staying active biking and running. Her favorite place to relax is sitting on the beach with a good book.

— CHAPTER 41 —

The Narrow Path

BY EMILY

I walk the narrow path. (Matthew 7:14) I thought I said "yes" to Jesus when I was 13.

"Yes, Jesus, you can love me."

But really, I said "yes" to Him when I was 16.

"Yes Jesus, I will love and LIVE for You."

My third point of decision came this year when I was 30. As I was walking on the beach having a conversation (a grumbling and complaining session) with the Lord, He said these words to me.

"You trusted Me as a child. Will you trust Me now as a woman?"

It's like all the choices, all the decisions that I had made in faith back as a teenager had taken me to this point. But now after 17 years of the narrow path, I was tackling deep realities of my heart. It kind of went like this ... I feel like I give MUCH and receive LITTLE. I feel like I do my best to "seek first the Kingdom," but I sure don't feel very "added to." (Matthew 6:33) I feel tired, weary of well doing. (Galatians 6:9) My marriage has been hard. Ministry has been hard. EVERYTHING has been hard; lots of bitter with a little bit of sweet. Lord, I know it's all worth it in theory, but is it really? WHAT ABOUT ME?!?!? I was mad, really. Discouraged. Disappointed. Fearful of the future. Fearful of His plan.

I felt like, as a teenager, I had put all my eggs in one basket. You know, like they say you're not supposed to do. Except the thing here is, I gave all my "eggs" to the Lord. Walking that white sandy beach in January, my heart was screaming out, "Lord!!! You're not being careful!!!" ... (with my eggs) ... I felt broken.

The narrow path — it's quite easy at times, but also so hard at times. I was 18, for just 18 days, when I got married. I had NO idea. NO idea. Marriage is, by far, the most difficult thing I have ever done. I married the man that the Lord had said my husband would be. Yes, it was an "arranged marriage." I was 17 when He told me I was going to marry this man. Let it be known that I wasn't looking for a husband when I was 17. God is crazy. You never know what He is going to do. My husband is wonderful, though; and even much better now than he was back in 1999 when we married. And I am much, much better too. Here's to 13 years of "iron sharpening iron." Cheers! (Proverbs 27:17)

My husband and I both have white skin and we both love Jesus. That's about where our similarities end. And even in loving Jesus, we both have a variety of ideas on how to go about living for Him. I often joke to myself that when we have children, they are going to praise Jesus that we had them later in our marriage, rather than sooner. Our home is a much happier place these days.

So I was talking about all those choices, all those decisions I made in faith back as a teenager. I was a junior in high school. I loved new things, new places, busyness, poetry, people watching. I was trying to get a plan around, since that's when schools and families, etc. start putting the pressure on. What are you going to do with your life? I wonder how many people are actually doing what they thought they had figured out when they were a junior in high school? Well, I was going to go to college in or near New York City. My aunt had taken me once and I absolutely loved it there. I would go to school for writing.

I had an English teacher that had really inspired me in writing. I also had a crush on him so he got me to do things out of my comfort zone like forensics team, which was a competition based on areas of public speaking, acting, reading and interpretation. It was the FIRST thing on the extracurricular list that I would not have signed up for. I still can't believe I did it. I was the English class editor. Everyone wanted me to proofread their papers before turning them in so they would get a better grade. I read books and books and books about writing. For a while, I got up early before school and wrote every morning. It was an exercise in your "voice," just writing whatever popped into your head. I loved writing.

So it was college in the Big Apple and I was going to go and be a writer. Here's the thing, though. When you commit to loving and living for Jesus, you don't get to live your plan. So before long, God ambushed me and I was living in Elkhart, Ind., not New York, N.Y. I was a receptionist answering phones at an insurance company, not a budding writer. I was at home married, not exploring life and the world.

However, this was not my plan going wrong, it was that I was following His plan, well the best that I could. I just wanted to please the Lord and do what He wanted me to. I abandoned myself to His plan.

So back on the beach, January 2012; I am still living in Elkhart, still a receptionist at the same insurance company, and thankfully, still married. But, walking on that beach that day with the wind pressing against my face, I felt like I had put all my chips in, bet it all on God ... and lost. I felt empty. But there was His voice.

"You trusted Me as a child. Will you trust Me now as a woman?"

So I'm walking, walking and I see something dark green down in the white sand. I picked it up and all I could see on it was, "In God We Trust." This quarter had been in the ocean so long, it was thin and green, and it happened to wash up on shore right then as I was walking by. I love it when God "happens" to me. He loves me. He does.

It's recorded in the book of John about a time that Jesus said some things that were very offensive to many who followed Him. In John 6:66 ESV it says,

> After this many of his disciples turned back and no longer walked with him.

I think there are different times, different seasons, and in many different situations where we are tested. Will I be offended with the Lord? Will I turn back? Will I walk away?

I recently read this in a blog by John Eldredge of "Ransomed Heart."

> "There is nothing like suffering to wreak havoc in your relationship with God. The damage pain does to our relationship with Jesus is often far, far worse than the pain itself.
>
> Every time I turned to Jesus in the midst of one episode of heartache then another, every single time I turned to Him, the first thing He would say was, 'Love me.' At first it surprised me — aren't You supposed to say You love me? I'm the one who's hurting here. But somehow, instinctively, I knew what He meant, knew what He was after. "Love Me now, in this — not for this, but in this." (emphasis mine). And those words have been a rescue.
>
> Here's why: Pain causes us to pull away from God. At the very moment we need Him most, we pull back. Our soul withdraws, like a snail into its shell. Then you not only have the heartache,

you have 'lost' God for a while too. Desolation on top of suffering. Sometimes it takes months, even years to recover the relationship. Jesus was rescuing me from that cycle by telling me to love Him now, right in the midst of the pain.

On a soul level, when I love God in this place, it opens my heart and soul back up to Him right where I need Him most, right in the center of the pain. Too often what we cry out for is understanding — 'why, God?' But I've learned over the years that when you are in the midst of the suffering, you don't often get understanding, and frankly, you don't need understanding — you need God.

And so, dear friends, I wanted to pass this along to you, for it has been a great help to me. Love Jesus, right there, right in the midst of the pain. Just start telling Him you love Him, right where you are hurting. For as you do, it enables your heart to open back up to Him, it enables Him to come to you in this very place. And it is Jesus that we need. Desperately." [7]

That short little blog ministered to me so much. I hope it ministered to you just now.

So back to the Bible, in the book of John, Jesus says to His 12 disciples, "Do you want to go away as well?" And it says that Simon Peter answered Him, "Lord, to whom shall we go? You have the words of eternal life, and we have believed, and have come to know, that You are the Holy One of God."

So that's it friends, back on the beach. Where else would I go? If I quit everything, what else would I do? I was too embarrassed to scream at the top of my lungs (even though there was no one around) but in my spirit I cried out to the Lord.

"YES!!!!!!!!!!!!!!!!!!!" I said, "Yes. Yes I will trust You. Yes. I will keep walking this narrow path, putting one foot in front of the other, doing my best to walk in a manner worthy of the calling. (1 Thessalonians 2:12) Yes. I will trust You with my heart."

Just writing this now makes me feel a bit anxious inside. That goes to show how much further I have to go, how much more I need to know His love for me, to know Him in my heart, and not just in my head. Pray for me. Really. Please pray for me to know Him more.

This is the story of my narrow path. May you find joy and peace in your own journey. He is the true treasure. He is the true prize. This is not the end of the story.

For now we see in a mirror dimly, but then face to face. Now

I know in part; then I shall know fully, even as I have been fully known. So now faith, hope, and love abide, these three; but the greatest of these is love. 1Corinthians 13:12-13 ESV

Emily grew up in Michigan with a sweet and joyful nature. Since 1999 when she married, she and her husband have partnered together in their calling to hear and minister the voice of God and to teach, train and equip others to do the same. Emma loves going new places, trying new things, walking on any beach, sitting around crackling campfires, hiking and taking hot showers. She adores her family, cuddling with her husband, and time spent with good friends.

— CHAPTER 42 —

Living an Authentic Life in the Image of God

BY ELIZABETH

"Today the world will ask you who you are,
And if you do not know, the world will tell you."
- Attributed to Carl Jung

"Daughter, you took a risk trusting me, and now you're
healed and whole. Live well, live blessed!"
- Jesus to the woman who had been hemorrhaging for 12
years. Luke 8:48 MSG

"Take a look at Beth: This is a perfect example of how Christian girls should not dress."

"Why do you ask so many questions? This is what all Christians believe."

"We can't let you teach Sunday school anymore because women can't be in authority over men."

"Does your husband let you read books like that?"

"In this church, women can make food for shut-ins, teach VBS and visit the sick."

"Why don't you have kids, yet? Why do you want a career?"

I can still physically feel the anger, shame and humiliation that were a part of each of these conversations. In each encounter and dialogue in at least 15 of the more than 30 years of my life within the Christian faith, I learned that who I was as a person — and as a woman — was unacceptable to God because I did not fit the mold of the silent, invisible, powerless, breeding ideal of Christian womanhood. This dislocation of my self-identity taught me that in the eyes of the church (God!) I was some kind of "mutant" because my questioning, outspoken and extroverted self did not fit the social construction of the Christian feminine ideal. God made me an outcast and I spent 15 years of my life searching for an identity and a place to fit. This is where I have been.

This story traces my present-moment, ongoing journey from hunger to wholeness as I am claiming my identity as a Christian feminist. My spiritual journey includes living from a segmented, fragmented and false identity to becoming a woman who is more unified — and hopefully authentic — through living as a disciple of Jesus Christ. While I have listened to the many voices that have lied about who I am — and about who we are as women — I am coming to believe the voice of the One who has called me to belong to Him, the One who is bringing all my exiled selves home.

I am not alone in this struggle. This fragmentation of self is commonplace. I teach in a Christian college in the Midwest and have close relationships with several female students. Every week, I encounter conversations revolving around the pain of the past, physical and sexual abuse, desire to marry and confusion about God's will. One student said that, "I always thought that God just liked guys better." I am stunned that the same toxic message about women's inferiority that had poisoned my life for so long is still around.

As women learn who we are in the face of a fundamental point of view about the "creation order" of male dominance and female subordination, the messages we receive about our roles strongly influence our understanding of who we are as disciples, selves, church participants, daughters, students, friends, girlfriends, women and what we should expect in the future as workers, wives, singles and mothers.

I still wonder why women never hear the powerful truth that they — along with men — bear God's image and are charged to create and replenish the earth. Women who lack this understanding are handicapped in their ability to offer God their lives and their full service for God's purpose. As a result, half of the church is muted while women experience alienation from themselves, God, and the world as we struggle to find the place to exist between Christian and secular culture and in private and public spheres. Many experience contradictions and disconnection from the very institutions that represent the One who can bring abundant life (John 10:10). Frustrated, some women leave the faith; others stay and are silent.

In my own life, as I encountered a social expectation or message that contradicted my true self, then I had to chose to go against the way things are "supposed to be" and risk disapproval, or hide my true feelings and present a self to others that would play in the theatre of life. I learned that to survive, I had to separate who I was from my identity as a woman. This resulted in the divorce of my mind from my emotions; my body became an enemy to control; and my real life moved from the God who refused to like me to the work I could perform and the money I could earn.

Many experiences compose the story of my journey with the joys and conflicts of my life as a Christian and a woman. I learned and understood that to survive within the church and "with God," I had to hide the best parts of myself behind masks I would create to be socially acceptable and as a means to cope with all the contradictions.

The Mask of Family

My nuclear family was traditional with my mom at home and my dad the bread winner. I was close to them, but learned that being a woman meant that there were limits on my life, as I observed my mother's traditional life and as most of their hopes and dreams were lavished on my elder brother. His future, his academic achievement and choice of marriage partners were the locus of my parents' parenting. As a young girl, my mother loved me and my father ignored me. I figured that my brother was the smart one and I was the social one. In school, I made many friends and created an imaginary world where I was heard and safe. I spent much time writing short stories and rewriting other stories I saw on television to include myself as an active female character.

My parents came to Christ when I was in middle school and this changed many things in our home for the better. My parents' marriage improved and equalized. My father involved me in his work while I was in high school and our relationship has changed for the better. My mother and I are very close and she has a much stronger voice than she had in my childhood. The earlier understanding of a woman's secondary role, my own invisibility within my family and the power relationships of marriage were some of my early understandings that I came to believe about gender.

The Mask of Appearance

I became a Christian in high school at a Bible youth camp and experienced the magnificent love of Christ. I knew that I was forgiven, accepted and loved. For me this was a real and overwhelming experience. Our family attended a very traditional church at this time. It was here that I began to learn that I was unacceptable to God and needed to be reformed. My youth pastor singled me out in front of others as an example of how young Christian women should not dress (mini skirts) and act. He had some real issues of his own, but being publicly condemned by a pastor at 15 was a real blow to my self esteem. This overemphasis on the biblical passages about female modesty and silence gave me mixed messages about my body and brain. This was the first point of conflict and fragmentation: While it was good to try and be pretty, it was bad to look too good.

The Mask of Stupidity

A second message from church was that asking questions in Sunday school was not acceptable for girls — we were supposed to accept what we were taught at face value. My Sunday school teacher asked me to stop asking questions and just believe. The narrative viruses of The "Total Woman" and Bill Gothard's "Basic Youth Conflicts" infected my church. God wanted women to be silent, obey and breed. Two saving graces for me were Young Life and a Bible study in the home of one of my public high school teachers that had us reading books like "Mere Christianity." It was there that I found that it was okay to be a Christian who had a brain. Still, the toxic image, the limitations for female achievement, was planted in my mind. It was acceptable to be smart, not *too* smart.

The Mask of Thinness

Related to the issues of the body and modesty were the issue of my size and weight. I dated a few boys in high school and one told me to lose some weight (I was 5'5" and weighed about 130 pounds). In response, I dieted and exercised excessively, lost 10 pounds, then 20, then 30. I received so many compliments on my skinny self that I just kept going. I stopped having periods. I wouldn't take communion in church because of the calories. I bottomed out at about 105 pounds, but was on the road to having an eating disorder. I separated my God concepts from my body, because God didn't like my female body very much, but young men did. I often dressed in tight clothes for this attention and affirmation.

The Mask of a Fractured Self

I started reading second wave, secular feminists in the '70s and '80s, searching for some kind of validation of being female ("Ms." magazine, "The Second Sex," "The Female Eunuch" and "The Women's Room"). Here, I found kindred spirits that called for women to be equal, and yet the anger at Christianity seemed too dangerous for me to name as my own. It seemed that the push towards a career, financial independence and a life without children was the golden ticket to navigating the waters of being female. Besides, I was not domestic or beautiful, but I was smart. I went with my brain, trying to play the cards dealt by life. I placed my Christian walk in a separate space in my heart and my growing "feminism" in another place to survive. Fragmentation of self was becoming a way of being in the world.

The Mask of Marriage as a Straightjacket

Life at college was rewarding and largely neutral where these issues were concerned. I found some unity and balance. My big problem was that I truly loved my boyfriend (Donald), but marriage was unthinkable because it would mean that I would cease to exist and have to be some kind of fake "total woman." Here, I knew that if I gave in to a relationship and to marriage that I would have to disappear. Finally, as I graduated with honors, I agreed to marry, but wrote my own vows to "honor Donald as a man and a human being" because they couldn't possibly be the same thing.

Off with One Mask and On with Another

While starting as a young, married career woman, my fragmentation was in full force. I read everything I could get my hands on concerning women's issues and Christianity, and things didn't look too promising. While my marriage was egalitarian, I had many encounters with ministers — one of whom wouldn't let me teach adult Sunday school because one man wanted to attend the class — and I finally "resigned" as a Christian (I did this in a Bible study), because God clearly did not like me the way he created me. The best things in me — my mind, my passion, my ambition — God did not want and I was sick of all the game playing and mask wearing.

I removed the mask of being a Christian and exchanged it for a briefcase and wool suit. While I was a failure with God, I was successful at my work in advertising and public relations (not-for-profit and agency work). It was here I decided to find my validation. Finally at age 29, I started an ad agency with three male co-workers who were anything but Christian. I did this with the full support of my husband.

At this time we were attending a United Methodist Church, in part because they are not afraid of women. But in my heart, my resignation from Christianity was in force. I also started smoking and drinking to maintain the pace, stay thin and win the approval of these men who wanted the sales I made (my revenue output was strong), but refused to make me a full partner as per our agreement. I put up with unbelievable abuse from two of these partners and yet stayed with it because my entire self-esteem was at stake. I learned that to get along with men in the workplace, I had to swear, speak in short sentences that discussed the bottom line, look good and totally suppress any emotion. Donald and I lived with this fragmented limbo for three years.

The Purgation of Pregnancy

At 31, the unthinkable happened. I was pregnant! I was in an utter crisis and did not know what to do. Donald and I were having some issues, and I knew if I had a baby, my life would be over. I would become fat, invisible and dependent. I considered not going through with the pregnancy, but knew that I could not have an abortion, because that would mean that there is no hope. God was on another planet laughing at me for finally getting caught by being female. The masks were off and I was exposed to the worst thing that could happen. But then it wasn't. Ironically, becoming a mother was the starting point for my reunification and encounter with grace and wholeness in Christ.

How Jesus Began to Put Me Together

I now speak of a process that I am in the middle of — for every step on the road that I take forward on the journey to wholeness — there is always one or two backwards that I take back from the gravitational pull of fragmentation. However, it is in listening to the voice of Christ in the dialogue with the Bible and other texts, and in the dialogue with life itself in the form of my family, women friends and church community that I am coming to understand that the many experiences I have had are not from God, but were truly lies from the enemy.

With the experience of having a child, a "baby woman," as I called her, came the realization that when I let go of God, God did not let go of me. My husband and I got some counseling and my inner focus shifted from living for my job. Our marriage started working well again as we adjusted to the new challenge of becoming parents after so many years. I had Kaitlin 'Grace' and continued to work full time in the agency. Two years later, after trying to balance these two modes of life, I had a second daughter, Holly Carolyn. Finally, with a 2-year-old and a newborn, I came home — reluctantly — and left the agency to the one remaining partner who actually turned out to be a decent human being. My integration had started through my bewildered acceptance of my body's ability to have children, and the realization that a life built on endless deadlines and pressure was no longer satisfying, as if it ever really was.

As I came home, I was dislocated and depressed. Working was all I ever knew and being with children was foreign to me. Rescue came in the form of a female friend who lived in our neighborhood. She introduced me to the mysteries of little kids and introduced me to a community of other women with young children at our church. These women were smart and at home. I was amazed! I cautiously started talking about my experiences, which many of them did not share. But, they listened anyway and I confronted the sin of my own bias against stay-at-home mothers.

Next, I attended a Walk to Emmaus, a retreat weekend sponsored by the United Methodist Church to give its leaders a fresh experience of Christianity. This experience completely blew me away as I re-encountered the Christ that I first came to know in high school before the church tried to "fix me." I experienced some healing from the past and encountered the grace of the risen Christ. I could now name the grace that kept me from destroying myself, my marriage and my children as "prevenient grace," the grace that went before me as I journeyed into fragmentation. My renewed hunger for scripture grew as I began anew to read the Bible again for the first time.

I now read scripture from the standpoint of the risen Christ: his work, person, teachings of Jesus of Nazareth. Many feminist concerns about scripture and the roles of women can be properly laid to rest with a biblical view that understands how Christ came to restore the sons and daughters of God to right standing with God, each other and ourselves. Christ came to restore the imago Dei that was lost in the beginning.

The Truth that Frees the Captive Daughters of God

The Bible is replete with stories of how God came to set people free. Both men and women bear the image of God, they both are given the tasks of stewardship, and that there is no gender politics or hierarchy as they relate to God and each other. In the original plan of God, men and women are created for divine connection, cooperation and costewardship, community, communication and freely chosen love.

The most compelling biblical texts for me are those where Jesus interacted with women and, in spite of the patriarchy of his day, treated them as equals, individuals, disciples, colleagues and friends. In short, in his teachings and the example of His life, Jesus modeled the restorative relationship as it was intended: Jesus is a feminist. In Matthew 19, when asked about divorce, Jesus reaffirms the imago Dei of women as well as men and criticizes the custom that treats women as disposable property.

The fact that Jesus is a feminist affirms my place as a feminist, quest for unification of my self and search for understanding my identity as imagebearer. This feminist dialogue with scripture continues as the final — and ongoing — step towards praxis is explored. I seek to understand my place as an imagebearer of God and to bring this understanding of what this means to my relationship with God, my husband and daughters, my teachers and students, my church and community — and to my re-emerging self. My theological grounding for how this works is based on a reading of Matthew 16, as Peter acknowledges who Christ is and Jesus, in turn, tells Peter who He is.

I would like to be able to say that I am now living a happily-ever-after life filled with unity and authentic joy. This would be another lie and another mask: the lie that I have arrived at the final destination or achieved feminist karma. Like the Christian story that lives within the tensions of the already-happened and not-yet reality of Christ's victory, my life moves between the poles of progress and regress. Yet, things are better. Many of the masks are gone, and many are gently being removed.

My relationship with God is moving toward a greater place of trust. I relate to God through the lens of Jesus and experience with God's grace, forgiveness and faithfulness. My relationship with myself is the locus of most of my conflict. With my many roles as wife, daughter, mother, professor, administrator, student, writer, I am still tempted to judge my worth by my usefulness. Yet, I am more at peace than ever. My times of insecurity and unbalance do not come as often or last as long. This is better. I do struggle with accepting changes to my middle-aged body and face, yet like the fact that I am remaining healthy through a reasonable diet and exercise. I am starting to accept that Christ accepts me, which theologian Paul Tillich says is the most difficult task of the spiritual life.

My relationship with my husband has never been better as the masks I have always worn for self-protection are largely gone. It is through his faithfulness and acceptance that I have come to believe in God's faithfulness and acceptance. My adult daughters are women and friends I am proud to know.

My relationship with my students, particularly my female students, is one place where I try to be open and affirm their uniqueness as God's daughters. I hope when the world asks them who they are, they will each have an answer of their own as image-bearers of God. Time will tell. As for me, I am whole as Christian, feminist, wife, mother, teacher and scholar.

Elizabeth came to know Jesus in high school, left the faith when teaching about women's roles left her feeling like God really did not like her very much. Through college, career and marriage, she found more of a home in her career in public relations and marketing. With the birth of her daughters, the grace of Clay United Methodist Church, Elizabeth is surprised to be loved by God. She is a communicator professor who encourages Bethel College students to find their voices and expression of image-bearers of God.

Epilogue

As you already know, Jaimee and I felt the Lord tell us to write this book. The other thing that we felt the Lord promoting us to do was to coordinate a conference for women where they would share their stories with one another.

The conference drew close to 250 women from four nearby states. We had 23 women from 15 different churches on the ministry team and the conference itself drew in women from 27 different churches within the region. There were Catholic women, Amish women, African American and Caucasian; there were young women and older women. To summarize, there was unity in the body. We even had a few women fly in from California to support one of the speakers that was undergoing chemotherapy at the time. She received a standing ovation. Before the conference, we had many people encouraging us.

We also had a couple of people email us that were, let's say, doubtful about the success of the conference. One person thought that we might be setting up the participants for disappointment by calling it a healing conference. What if God didn't show up?

On the journey to the conference, Jaimee and I learned a valuable lesson. It was simple. We are not God and we are not responsible for healing anyone. He told us to have the conference and we believed He would show up. This leads into another question. What is healing supposed to look like? I believe that through my experience in interviewing the women and my trust in God's work, that healing was to look like anything God wanted it to look like. Every woman at the conference had a different need. Some women needed to hear a fresh word from God, others needed to know that there were women in this area that share similar stories as them, others needed someone to put their arms around them to tell them everything was going to be OK and still others needed to shout and dance.

On that day, God met every need. It was great to know that no person had to carry the burden of having to fix anybody. Afterwards, we received emails and phone calls from women telling us what Jesus did for them at the conference. Jaimee and I were simply thankful for listening to God's voice, and that's just the way we liked it. God receiving all the glory!

An Impactful Story

I met an Amish woman, who currently lives in a small Indiana town. She heard me talk about the woman in Mark 5 at the conference and was greatly moved. At the end of the conference she came up to me and embraced me and began to cry. She then invited me to her home and shared her story.

She was violently abused by her husband and had to be relocated for her own safety. After she fled her community, she moved to a new community and received further persecution. A group of bishops and elders from her old community visited her new location and told the community there to shun her too. This woman was exiled and was not allowed to participate in worship or any other gatherings.

The greatest part of her story was through all this heartache, she trusted God and went deeper in her relationship with Him. She could have given up or become bitter, but she did just the opposite.

When we first started writing this book, I had no idea how much the stories of these women would impact me. While I can't speak about Jaimee's experience, for me, hearing these women's stories has set me free from wrong thoughts of how I see God, how He chooses to heal and how much He loves His people — especially women. In fact, I believe that's one of the Kingdom messages in Mark 5.

That story was not only about a woman who touches the hem of Jesus' garment and finds her identity and place back into society. The Kingdom components of the story speak about Jesus and His authority and the power to bring the Kingdom of God here on earth. Jesus affirms the woman by calling her daughter (Mark 5:34) and she becomes a member of the community of believers.

Priceless Experience

For Jaimee and I, we were humbled by the response of the women and the support of others: Pastor Edgar Cabello (Southgate Church), Pastor Ricardo Taylor (Mt. Carmel Missionary Baptist Church), Bob Deering (Voice Ministries), Emily Miller (Voice Ministries), Michiana Prayer Network (Ellen Stanley), Shelly Cowling (Clay United Methodist Church), Zion Missionary Church and professors from Bethel College: Chad Meister, Ph.D., and David McCabe Ph.D. We are grateful that this wasn't about a denomination, but about the Kingdom of believers working together in unity to glorify God.

Another valuable lesson we both learned was to trust the Holy Spirit in everything that He has set for us to do, and to let others in the body of Christ rally around and bring their talents to help. Jaimee has a gift for writing and communicating and she loves people. I have a gift to unite people of different backgrounds, and I enjoy speaking and helping people find their identity in Christ. God used our natural gifts and turned them into ministry — tools used for healing women.

In the future, we hope to bring women together in the region to share their story with other women in formal and informal settings. We would like to see women come together to heal each other through the power of their stories so that God may be glorified.

Joan McClendon

End Notes

1. Adam Clarke Commentary: woman's remedies.
    www.studylight.org/com/acc/view.cgi?book=mr&chapter=005

2. Ralph Gower. The New Manners and Customs of Bible Times
    (Chicago: Moody Press, 1987), 170-171

3. The Witness Protection Program.
    www.usmarshals.gov/duties/factsheets/witsec-2011.pdf

4. Ralph Gower. The New Manners and Customs of Bible Times
    (Chicago: Moody Press, 1987),346

5. Define Community.
    www.merriam-webster.com/dictionary/community

6. Alisa's story.
    www.spellbinders.org/docs/PortraitOfPeace.pdf

7. Emily's story
    www.ransomedheart.com/blogs/john/loving-jesus-pain

About the Authors

Joan McClendon

A longtime resident of South Bend, Joan's passion is empowering women to find their identity in Christ and promoting the gospel through the power of testimonies. A former youth pastor, she has served at the St. Joseph County Jail and through the JAG program at Adams High School mentoring young women in South Bend, Ind. She also coaches girls track for Holy Cross and St. Matthew's schools. Joan has a master of ministries degree and is currently working on her second master of arts in theological studies at Bethel College in Mishawaka, Ind. She is married to her college sweetheart, Cary, of 20 years. They have two children, Joshua, 16 and Moriah, 14.

Jaimee Bingle

Jaimee is a newlywed living in Mishawaka, Ind. with her wonderful husband, Nathan. Her heart is to help others hear the voice of God, training others in the prophetic to build up the body of Christ. Currently, she works as the director of marketing and communications at Bethel College. She and her husband enjoy travelling, reading books and eating good food together.

We invite you to visit our website: *LifeontheFringe.org*

- Share your testimony of healing and read other women's testimonies
- Read our blog
- Discover resources for your healing
- Contact the authors about speaking to your organization or group

Made in the USA
Lexington, KY
10 September 2018